"Hastings exhorts the fragmented American Protestant communities to hold fast to the vision of unity in Christ incarnate. . . . Inspired by the diverse global Christian communities, he reflects on how this vision might lead to the renewed catechesis of 'worship,' 'witness,' and 'wonder as ways Christians participate with a sense of common cause in the mission of the God of love and life.'"

—**Haruko Nawata Ward**, Columbia Theological Seminary

"Tom Hastings is an important mentor and guiding light in Christian education, mission studies, and theology. This book is a gem, refracting with wisdom and care ways for us to grow in Christ, creating beauty and doing justice in a fragmented time for the church and the world."

—**Makoto Fujimura**, artist, and
Haejin Shim Fujimura, justice advocate

"No one interested in the progress of the churches in the Majority World can afford to miss this wonderful book. Backed by years of experience as a teaching missionary and a scholar, Tom Hastings pulls together the fruits of a lifetime. The reader will be inspired anew by wonder and witness for the sake of mission and worship. Horizons will be expanded and hope renewed by the insights that are here encountered."

—**George Hunsinger**, Princeton Theological Seminary

"Drawing on his decades-long experiences as an American practical theologian serving in Japanese contexts, Hastings is ideally equipped to offer discernment and encouragement to those facing the enormous challenges of Christian formation and mission. . . . Borne of a brilliant reading of Scripture, tradition, and mission theology, Hastings's wisdom will enrich the global church, whether in India, Indonesia, or Indiana."

—**Jacob Cherian**, Southern Asia Bible College

"The combination of clarity and brilliance in this book is remarkable. . . . This book is a must-read for leaders who are thinking about the transformation of the church in a post-pandemic, polarized, and rapidly secularizing world. . . . Drawing on theology and the social sciences, he invites leaders to view worship, witness, and wonder as forms of participation in the mission of Christ through the Holy Spirit. Fresh, challenging, and inspiring."

—**Richard R. Osmer**, Princeton Theological Seminary, emeritus

Worshiping, Witnessing, and Wondering

Cover: "The Great Commission" by Nalini Jayasuriya (1927–2014)

Mixed Media on Canvas, 28" x 53". Used with permission of the Overseas Ministries Study Center at Princeton Theological Seminary.

"To me, the Great Commission is much more than the words that Jesus spoke to the twelve. So, I have tried to suggest the Power that had to sweep through humanity and through Time, transcending all thought and illumining all experience. So, Christ makes a Statement and an Offering, a Statement of the Abiding Holy Spirit in the form of a Dove, and the Offering of his Life in the symbol of the Cup. This is not a portrait of the young vibrant giver of the Gospels, but an almost elusive vision of a spiritual Presence—a Presence eternally renewing."

Nalini Jayasuriya

OMSC Artist in Residence 2001–2003

May 23, 2002

3.29.2022

Dear Jacq,

Worshiping, Witnessing, and Wondering

Christian Wisdom for Participation in the Mission of God

With thanks for your leadership and ministry!

Thomas John Hastings

Every blessing,

Tom

CASCADE *Books* • Eugene, Oregon

WORSHIPING, WITNESSING, AND WONDERING
Christian Wisdom for Participation in the Mission of God

Cascade Books
An Imprint of Wipf and Stock Publishers
199 W. 8th Ave., Suite 3
Eugene, OR 97401

www.wipfandstock.com

PAPERBACK ISBN: 978-1-6667-2327-4
HARDCOVER ISBN: 978-1-6667-2002-0
EBOOK ISBN: 978-1-6667-2003-7

Cataloguing-in-Publication data:

Names: Hastings, Thomas John, author.

Title: Worshiping, witnessing, and wondering : christian wisdom for participation in the mission of God / by Thomas John Hastings.

Description: Eugene, OR : Cascade Books, 2022 | Includes bibliographical references.

Identifiers: ISBN 978-1-6667-2327-4 (paperback) | ISBN 978-1-6667-2002-0 (hardcover) | ISBN 978-1-6667-2003-7 (ebook)

Subjects: LCSH: Mission of the church. | Mission of the church—Biblical teaching. | Missions. | Missions—History. | Missions—Biblical teaching.

Classification: BV2061.3 .H37 2022 (print) | BV2061.3 .H37 (ebook)

02/02/22

I dedicate what follows to all those who have been part of classes and seminars I have led over the past forty years—young and not so young, lay and ordained, theologians and scholars from non-theological fields, Christians and friends of other faith traditions and those of no faith tradition, students from all over the world. And I extend this dedication to those with whom I have shared the joys and challenges of common life; namely, Carol, our four children, eight grandchildren, extended family, and dear friends in the States, in Japan, and on every continent. In ways you will never know, you have all encouraged me to worship, to witness, and to wonder.

Worldly wisdom thinks that love is a relationship between one human being and another. Christianity teaches that love is a relationship between: persons-God-persons, that is, that God is the middle term.

—Søren Kierkegaard, *Works of Love*

Contents

Introduction

KIERKEGAARD THREW DOWN THE gauntlet for followers of Jesus when he wrote in his journal, "The majority of people are subjective toward themselves and objective toward all others—terribly objective sometimes—but the real task is to be objective toward oneself and subjective toward all others."[1] Kierkegaard is touching here on the ultimate goal of lives "hidden with Christ in God" (Col 3:3b), lives characterized by a gradual turning from self-centeredness to self-giving and patterned after the One confessed to be fully human and fully God. This paradoxical confession apprehends in the mission of God in Jesus Christ a unique harmony between God and humanity, a harmony that, through the lens of the enigmatic events of cross and resurrection, has led followers across the ages to confess Jesus as Christ and as Lord. In the humanity of Jesus Christ, God embodies, sanctifies, and redeems all dimensions of human life (biological, material, personal, sociopolitical, and cultural). When teaching on the incarnation, I like to say, "God has been here in person, not as some alien visitor from a faraway planet, but as one of us—and that makes all the difference."

At the same time, it seems clear that the confession of the unity of divinity and humanity in Jesus Christ was far from a *fait accompli* for the first followers of the Way. Indeed, the Synoptic Gospels show Jesus rejecting divine ascriptions at every turn. And Paul quotes an early Christian hymn that confesses the divinity of Christ in a somewhat reticent, or "minor," key, inviting readers to

1. Kierkegaard, *Journals*, 212–13.

sing along: "Though he was in the form of God, he did not regard equality with God as something to be exploited, but emptied himself, taking the form of a slave, being born in human likeness" (Phil 2:6–7). It is easy to forget that it took the churches in the Roman Empire several centuries of worshiping God, witnessing to God's love for all, and wondering about—through hearing, studying, and interrogating—the Gospel that was scandalous to Jews and foolish to Greeks (1 Cor 1:23), to land on a nonbiblical term, *homoousion* ("same in essence"), to depict the immanent triune relations of the Father, Son, and Holy Spirit, and later to confess the "impossible possibility" of a perfect unity of the divine and human "in two natures, without confusion, without change, without division, without separation" (Chalcedon, 451 CE).

Apart from stories such as Jesus' birth, baptism, and transfiguration, the divinity of Jesus Christ is embedded in Gospel narratives centered on the mission or ministry of a human being, albeit a very extraordinary one. As the Swiss Reformer John Calvin puts it, Jesus Christ comes to us "clothed with his Gospel."[2] If it had been otherwise, that is, if Scripture had provided no stories about Jesus but only abstract declarations of his divinity, we may well admire him from a great distance, but we would not be so drawn to and so disturbed by his extraordinary humanity. So, what is it about Jesus clothed with his Gospel that draws us? Again, precisely because our lives are so unlike the life we encounter in the Gospels, Kierkegaard points to the humanity of Jesus as the sign of the "eternal difference between Christ and every Christian."[3]

For Christians, who, following Kierkegaard, acknowledge the infinite qualitative distinction between time and eternity and between God and humanity, the lifelong task of turning and turning "till we come round right" is given clear direction by the humanity of Jesus. We might picture Jesus clothed in his Gospel as the true north to which we are forever turning. At our best moments, we know ourselves as those who have been invited to participate in Jesus' intimate relation to the One he called "Abba"

2. Calvin, *Institutes* 3.2.6.

3. Kierkegaard, *Works of Love*, 108.

and to love others out of this knowledge of being beloved. Yet, given our inclination to self- and group-centeredness and to self- and group-deception, sometimes we wonder whether it is really possible for us to love God and neighbor in the way of Jesus, and to grasp that we, thanks to him, are fully welcomed and embraced by a loving and holy God. Especially considering what we have learned from biological evolution, genetics, and culture, we sometimes may wonder whether we are fated to be, on balance, full of ourselves and oblivious to others?

We come, then, to the question of whether there may be ways to foster growth in the grace of being "objective toward oneself and subjective toward all others." Following Calvin, Kierkegaard, Barth, and other critical realists, my view is that we will always be novices in the school of faith, hope, and love, having to begin again and again at the beginning, making slow, imperceptible progress, while also regressing from time to time, sometimes in egregious ways. The PC(USA)'s *Belonging to God: A First Catechism* asks, "Don't I have to be good for God to love me?" and answers, "No. God loves me in spite of all I do wrong."[4] If this simple question faithfully expresses a bedrock truth about God and human beings, should we not greatly rejoice that growth in the self-giving way of Jesus must be made possible only by the grace of God? And if growth in divine grace is indeed a possibility, theologians must have a sacred obligation to try to discern the contours of communal and personal life grounded in the faith, hope, and love of Jesus Christ.

This brings us at last to the question I want to address in this book: *How might communities and persons of faith turn from self-centeredness to self-giving after the pattern of Jesus Christ?* Notice that I place the primary accent on communities and persons within communities rather than on individuals. The many reasons for this emphasis will become clearer as we proceed.

So here at the outset, I want to outline three complementary characteristics of communities marked by their participation in the mission of God in Jesus Christ. First, *worshiping:* participation

4. Approved by the 210th General Assembly (1998) of the Presbyterian Church (USA).

in the mission of God is nurtured by loving God within a community of faith that gathers regularly for worship. In the worship of God, we respond with heart, soul, mind, and strength to the divine call "to love the Lord your God" and, in spite of our regular failings, the divine assurance of being forgiven and loved is received and nurtured over a lifetime through regular participation in liturgies of Word and sacrament.

Second, *witnessing:* participation in the mission of God is nurtured by loving and caring for those we encounter in all spheres of life. We express God's love by loving others. Neighbor love is the moral shape of the Christian life. But the command to "love your neighbor as yourself" is tested through day-to-day interpersonal engagements in our families, with friends and neighbors, in our involvements in schools and workplaces, and in our participation in social, cultural, and political life. When, by the grace of God, we love and care for others, we give witness to the truth that all are equal bearers of the divine image and equally beloved by God.

Third, *wondering:* communities called to love God and neighbor in the way of Jesus Christ strengthen their participation in the mission of God by asking tough questions in the company of trusted friends in and beyond the community of faith. No one escapes the tragic limits, sorrows, and absurdities of life. But Christians read, study, and interrogate their sacred texts together, making theologies and music, literature, and art. Through activities that foster intellectual and aesthetic wonder, worshipers and witnesses engage in a process of learning, unlearning, and relearning over a lifetime of discipleship.

This book describes how I came to this postcritical perspective, which sees a life marked by worship, witness, and wonder, not only in harmony with the evolutionary endowments of perception, action, and cognition, and not only as well-attested habits of the corporate and personal dimensions of religious life, but as *a tripartite gestalt contingent on divine agency and mediated through participation in Jesus Christ in the power of the Holy Spirit.* Here, worship, witness, and wonder are not understood primarily as descriptors of discrete moral or social practices whose meaning can be grasped or whose performance enhanced by the help of philosophy or social science. Rather, I will describe worship, witness, and wonder as ways Christians participate with a sense of common cause in the mission of the God of love and life, who comes to us in Jesus Christ "clothed in his Gospel" and in the power of the Holy Spirit, who has been "poured out upon all flesh" (see Acts 2:17).

* * *

I approach the subject of receiving and handing on the Gospel of Jesus Christ out of a lifetime of ecumenical, intercultural missional engagements; please forgive now a brief personal introduction. While trained in the practical theological discipline of Christian education in the United States, I spent much of my career in Japan as a mission coworker of the Presbyterian Church (USA), teaching in church-related colleges and a seminary associated with our partner church, the United Church of Christ in Japan (UCCJ).[5]

Founded in 1941, the UCCJ is Japan's largest Protestant denomination, made up mainly of former Congregational, Methodist, Presbyterian, and Reformed bodies pioneered mostly by North American missionaries in the second half of the nineteenth century. In Japan, Protestantism is a tiny minority faith in a society where the overwhelming majority of people claim dual religious affiliation with Shintoism and Buddhism. After more than 160 years of considerable Japanese and foreign efforts, all Protestants combined represent only about one half of 1 percent of Japan's population. Along with Roman Catholics, Orthodox, and several other groups, Japan's Christians make up between 1 and 2 percent of the population.

While teaching mostly Japanese students from 1987 to 2008, I was also an active participant in the educational ministries of several Japanese-speaking and English-speaking congregations. In Kanazawa, I led a weekly intergenerational English Bible study at

5. Hokuriku Gakuin (1987–91), Seiwa (1993–95), Tokyo Union Theological Seminary (1995–2008), and International Christian University (1997–2000, as adjunct).

Wakakusa Church (UCCJ); in Kobe, I helped lead a weekly adult Bible study for ex-pats and Japanese at Kobe Union Church; and in Tokyo, I led a weekly midweek Bible study at West Tokyo Union Church for ex-pats and Japanese, as well as helping out in elementary, junior and senior high, and adult classes in our church school. While the participants in the Bible study in Kanazawa were all Japanese, the other settings included people from Australia, Canada, China, Germany, Great Britain, India, Japan, Philippines, Taiwan, and the United States. The participants belonged to a wide range of church traditions, including Anglican/Episcopal, Baptist, Evangelical, Lutheran, Mar Thoma, Mennonite, Methodist, Pentecostal, Presbyterian, Reformed, Roman Catholic, and UCCJ.

In addition to my teaching and church experience in Japan, during our "interpretation assignments" in the States, I had the opportunity to visit almost one hundred Presbyterian Church (USA) congregations, where I preached or led educational forums for children, youth, and adults. After returning to the United States in 2008, I was associate director and research fellow at Princeton's Center of Theological Inquiry (2008–12), led a three-year John Templeton Foundation grant on science and religion in Japan as senior research fellow at the Japan International Christian University Foundation (2012–15), completed a consultancy on chaplaincy in Christian colleges and universities in Asia with the United Board for Christian Higher Education in Asia (2015–16), and since 2016 have been executive director of the Overseas Ministries Study Center, formerly in New Haven and now at Princeton Theological Seminary. A cradle Catholic, I have been a Presbyterian since my twenties, and my approach to the subject of the church's educational ministries has been shaped, challenged, and enriched by more than thirty years of experience as an intercultural pastoral educator, administrator, and scholar.

I have constantly found myself searching for ways for our various cultural and church traditions to engage in mutual edification and, most especially, for ways that the experience of Japanese Christians may encourage Christians in the United States and vice versa. First of all, as I will point out from time to time, the missional situation[6] of the minority churches in Japan is analogous to that of the early churches of the Greco-Roman world. Furthermore, while Protestants represent a tiny religious minority in Japan, the missional situation of the UCCJ also resembles in some ways, albeit on a much smaller scale, the contemporary crisis facing the Presbyterian Church (USA) and other "mainline" Protestant churches in the United States. While there are notable exceptions on both sides of the Pacific, in both places congregations are facing a rapidly aging membership, finding it difficult to retain the children of their adult members and having trouble attracting and retaining new members. While these issues may be fruitfully analyzed vis-à-vis theories of modernization, globalization, or pluralism, I believe that these issues are also related to the basic theological confusion concerning educational ministries, which I have already described above as growth in love for God and neighbor and participation in the mission of God.[7]

* * *

I turn briefly now to the shape of the book. In chapter 1, I describe in general terms how Protestant churches in the United States today approach Christian education and formation. I argue that these churches are sharply divided into what I call subjectivist, activist, and objectivist orientations to Christian education and formation, and suggest the need for more synthetic ways of thinking to supplement analytic modes.

In chapter 2, I draw on the brilliant account by Old Testament scholar Walter Brueggemann of Israel's normative "ways of knowing" in the *ethos* of Torah, the *pathos* of the Prophets, and the *logos* of the Writings. I make some tentative connections between these

6. I use the phrase "missional situation" to characterize the experience of Christian communities as they seek to be faithful to the Gospel amid the tensions between church and culture.

7. The initial shape of this approach was worked out in Japanese writing and lectures while I was teaching practical theology (Christian education) at Tokyo Union Theological Seminary from 1995 to 2008. More recently, I have presented it in outline form in my chapter "Worshiping, Witnessing, and Wondering" in *Consensus and Conflict* (2019).

"ways" and the function of *didachē*, *kerygma*, and *paraenesis* in the faith communities "in front of"[8] the New Testament writings.

In the following three chapters, I tease out these biblical insights by examining sources associated with the ancient catechumenate. I explore how churches in the Roman Empire integrated liturgical initiation, moral exhortation, and prebaptismal catechesis. Chapter 3 considers what might be called the "implicit curriculum" of the ancient catechumenate; namely, participation in a rich range of liturgical practices through which Christian faith was imprinted on the hearts, minds, and bodies of new initiates. Dudley and Hilgert make a helpful distinction between early Christian *rituals of structure* (i.e., exclamations, hymns, creeds, prayers, preaching, offering, and the Lord's Day) and *rituals of mystery* (i.e., baptism and Eucharist).[9] The ancient catechumenate incorporated regular participation in the church's rituals of structure as a preparation for participation in the rituals of mystery. Encompassing a rich array of verbal, auditory, and physical actions, these rituals of structure strengthened both the communal identity of the church and the personal identity of members.

Chapter 4 contrasts the teaching of Christian ethics in the early second-century *Didache* with the Apostle Paul's approach to *paraenesis* in his letters. This contrast is instructive for churches today who overemphasize one way of knowing while neglecting others.

Chapter 5 examines how Christian minds and affections were formed through a deliberate educational process of initiation that integrated a designated period of catechetical teaching, centered on Scripture and a creed, with regular participation in the ritual practices of the community of faith.

8. I borrow this term from French philosopher Paul Ricoeur, who believed that "there is something like a world of the text that lies not behind the text but metaphorically in front of it as something to be explored by the interpreter's imagination. This is a world that we can think of ourselves as inhabiting" (*Stanford Encyclopedia of Philosophy*, s.v. "Ricoeur"). See Ricoeur, *Interpretation Theory*, 80–88.

9. Dudley and Hilgert, *New Testament Tensions and the Contemporary Church*, 135–66.

1

The "Culture Wars" and Protestant Educational Ministry Today

I BEGIN BY COMMENTING on how I see the confusion about educational ministries in the Protestant churches today. Imagine the following thought experiment. You and I are friends who reside in the biblical city of Babel just after the Lord has come down and "confused the language of all the earth" (Gen 11:9). Trapped within our distinct linguistic walls, we have suddenly lost all ability to communicate with each other. You try to speak, and I see your lips moving and feel the vibration of your voice tingling in my inner ear, but your words come across as so much gibberish. I then start to speak, but you have no idea what I am trying to say. In this post-Babel confusion, we cannot even communicate our puzzlement to each other, but we both know something has gone wrong. It feels like we are reliving our first encounter with a new language as infants or as foreigners.

In our frustration, we leave off words and test out facial expressions and gestures, but immediately we discover that even embodied speech has been confused. We are then plunged helplessly back into silence, separation, and frustration. We become increasingly irritated with our inability to articulate, share, and verify our intended meanings. Even though we are both conscious that we share a treasured memory of the pre-Babel world, we are now left to interpret those memories on our own, within our completely distinct language worlds. In the absence of any mutual attestation of our distinct interpretations of this pre-Babel history, the menacing specter of absolute atomization overshadows all hopes for a shared future. In this post-Babel world, hardened opinion replaces open-ended explorations of truth with a small "t"—the fallible kind of truth claims that both the sciences and humanities like theology rely on—and all that remains is an increasingly boisterous and nasty competition of self-interest and deepening misunderstanding. In this condition, we may succeed in passing on our personal prejudices to the next generation or to new initiates but, having lost any way to adjudicate the views of others beyond our individual linguistic and cultural silos, our transmission of what our particular group "knows" and "values" loses its richness, depth, and nuance. A menacing cloud hovers over this post-Babel world.

I suggest that this thought experiment about the confusion of tongues and the loss of consensus about the rich and broad tradition of Christian faith is one way to think about the crisis facing Protestant churches in North America today. In the churches and in our social media and cable news "echo chamber" culture, this loss of consensus has given birth to a fierce and seemingly irreconcilable rivalry between ideological camps. The breakup of the churches rooted in the Reformation into hardened factions on the right and the left has contributed both to the internal division and weakening of our communities of faith and to a coherent public witness. One might say that embattled North American Protestants are in peril of losing their last vestige of catholicity, which of course was a shared historical and cultural presupposition when this movement first emerged out of the reforms of the sixteenth century.[1]

The post-Babel Protestant churches divide up into three identifiable approaches to the Christian faith,[2] which may be called

1. The denomination in which I was ordained as a minister of Word and Sacrament, the Presbyterian Church (USA), continues to claim that it "give[s] witness to the faith of the Church catholic," along with identifying itself within the Reformed stream of the churches grounded in the Protestant Reformation (*Book of Order*, G-2.0300–2.0500).

2. These are noetic categories, not types, which are based on years of participation in and observation of Protestant congregations in the United States

subjectivist, activist, and objectivist orientations. What makes this situation so challenging for pastors and church educators is that all three of these orientations are often present within a single local congregation. These three faith styles, which may change dramatically for individuals over a lifetime, also reflect the increasingly fluid boundaries between individual identity and social belonging in postmodern societies.[3] As work in the sociology of religion has shown, the number of groups Americans have to choose from has grown, even while the demands of group belonging have declined. Furthermore, our fragmented groups are ideal ecosystems for the growth of what Robert Jay Lifton calls the "Protean self."[4]

As an intercultural pastoral educator who has spent much of my career in Japan, where Protestant Christianity was introduced only about 160 years ago, I have observed and struggled with the loss of Protestant consensus on both sides of the Pacific. In Japan and the United States, the fragmenting drift of the Protestant churches—and here I would include mainline, evangelical, Pentecostal-charismatic, and independent churches—into subjectivist, activist, and objectivist orientations is reflected in all areas of church life. While I will focus on how these divisions have affected the church's educational ministries and spiritual formation of children, youth, and adults, one could also examine this problematic by looking at approaches to preaching, pastoral care, mission, or evangelism. My particular interest is educational ministry and spiritual formation, because it is here that I see

---

and Japan, and through professional and personal interactions with Christians from countries in Africa, Asia, Latin America, the Middle East, and Oceania.

3. See Fowler, *Stages of Faith*; Fowler et al., *Life Maps*; and Dykstra and Parks, *Faith Development and Fowler*.

4. Lifton defines this term as follows: "We are becoming fluid and many-sided. Without quite realizing it, we have been evolving a sense of self appropriate to the restlessness and flux of our times. This mode of being differs radically from that of the past, and enables us to engage in continuous exploration and personal experiment. I use the term 'protean self' after Proteus, the Greek sea god of many forms" (Lifton, *Protean Self*, 1).

the key question of growth in the mission of God in Jesus Christ is dealt with most directly.[5]

In my participation in and reflection on the educational ministries of Protestant congregations in the United States and Japan, I have noticed the following three patterns that correspond to the subjectivist, activist, and objectivist orientations introduced above:

1. *Subjectivist orientation to educational ministries and spiritual growth*: Emphasis on the experiential, affective, intuitive, or mystical dimensions of faith (i.e., through individual religious experience, conversion, spiritual practices, etc.).
2. *Activist orientation*: Emphasis on the active or vocational dimension of Christian faith (i.e., through consciousness of and participation in contemporary movements seeking social justice, political reform, and peace).
3. *Objectivist orientation*: Emphasis on the cognitive or propositional dimensions of faith (i.e., through mastering a particular church tradition's interpretation of Scripture and/or doctrine, perhaps with the aid of confessions of faith and catechisms).

While each of these orientations finds support in Scripture and church tradition, I have observed that educational ministries in congregations tend to seize upon one core orientation, often to the relative neglect of the other two. Depending on the convictions of those in charge of educational ministries at any given time, there is a propensity for congregations to bounce around willy-nilly between the three core orientations. A neutral observer may get the impression that there is an irreconcilable conflict between subjectivists, who emphasize religious experience, conversion, or spirituality; activists, who stress awareness of and engagement in emancipatory social or political causes; and objectivists, who focus on biblical or doctrinal study according to a specific interpretive tradition. In North America today, cable

5. Here I mean not only the Sunday School or Church School, which are often administered and taught by laypeople, but all of the educative practices of a congregation, including confirmation classes, new member classes, youth ministries, Bible studies, or any other groups led by clergy and laypeople.

news and social media, which gleefully promote and profit from the "niche-centered culture wars" that pit the left and the right against each other, have exacerbated the rivalry between these three basic orientations to the Christian faith.[6] Conversely, in this era of "reality TV" politicians, cable newscasters, and the social media echo chamber, one wonders whether the bitter antagonism between these orientations within religious communities themselves may be one source for the bitter culture wars.

The claim I wish to make here is that the crisis of contemporary American Protestantism is due to a loss of an inherent, holistic interplay between so-called subjectivist, activist, and objectivist orientations to faith. In the face of the breakup of communities of faith into mutually exclusive camps, I find myself—and many others with whom I have worshiped, witnessed, and wondered—longing for some way to reintegrate the strengths of all three orientations into educational ministries. Perhaps, like all the king's horses and all the king's men who could not put Humpty Dumpty together again, the deep ideological rifts in today's churches are beyond healing. Or perhaps, in times such as the COVID-19 pandemic, the awareness of the glaring limitations of our human resources may lead us back again, as it has in many other crises across the generations, to broader, more hopeful horizons we may have overlooked.

For Christian educators, one such theological issue is the relation of divine revelation (Word) and divine agency (Act), an issue many North American practical theologians have overlooked.[7] My hope in this book is to bring the crisis concerning how Christians worship, witness, and wonder (*epistemological* questions) into conversation with how Christians participate in the mission of the triune God through Jesus Christ and in the power of the Holy Spirit (*theological* questions).

6. *Invitation to readers:* Paying particular attention to leaders and curricula, review your church's educational ministries over the past five, ten, or even twenty years to test whether or not my claim of an unresolved competition between subjectivist, activist, and objectivist orientations is substantiated in the life of your own congregation.

7. See Hastings, *Practical Theology and the One Body of Christ*.

The field of Christian education, only relatively recently coming under the rubric "practical theology" in the seminary curriculum, has been assisted since the rise of the religious education movement in the early twentieth century by groundbreaking findings in the "human sciences" of developmental, cognitive, and social psychology, and later by existentialism, critical social theory, and anthropology. While these disciplines gave the educators of the church fruitful insight into the learning process, human development, and important existential, biological, social, cultural, and political issues that attend educational practice, the serious theological reflection that should also be an integral aspect of this discipline has, with only a few notable exceptions, been absent and left mostly in the hands of biblical scholars or systematic theologians. Clearly, we know much more today about effective educational methodologies, self-realization, and the dynamics of initiation, enculturation, and oppression than we did one hundred years ago. However, there have been some negative consequences for educational ministry as the interpretation of Christian faith has been hotly contested, drifting into irreconcilable ideological battles between subjectivists, activists, and objectivists.

I want to stress again that, because each of these three faith styles reflects an important aspect of Christian tradition, each has something vital to contribute to the nurture of Christian communities today. Nevertheless, in our post-Babel world, the inability of Protestant subjectivists, activists, and objectivists to communicate with each other and the tendency for us to caricature each other has led to a tragic impoverishment in our understanding of what is at stake in Christian education and spiritual growth. For reasons that will become clearer as we proceed, I see worship, witness, and wonder as three complementary ways of participating in the mission of the triune God in the world.

At the same time, we need to recognize that, because of these bitter mutual antagonisms, *worship* is often cast either in terms of an individualistic spirituality, by those with a psychological bias, or as a matter of participation in morally laden, formational communal practices, by those with a sociological or anthropological bias. Furthermore, the public *witness* of loving one's neighbor is threatened by several complex factors, such as the privatization of religion, caricatures of religious actors in the media, and the social and political marginalization of the churches. Finally, the attitude of *wonder*, both in the apprehensive sense of awe and in the interrogative sense of "I wonder . . ." that rightly attends the precarious business of handing on and receiving the Gospel, is undermined by literalism or propositionalism, on the one hand, or on the other, by the professionalization of the fields of biblical studies and systematic theology and their increasing detachment from congregational life. Finally, we should recognize that the former "mainline" churches are no longer at the center of social, cultural, or political life.[8] Joseph Small describes this situation well.

> The growing distance between North American culture and the church, and especially of the old mainline churches, is evident in numerous quantifiable ways. Mainline Protestant churches have experienced precipitous declines in membership, while denominational structures wither for lack of funds . . . The large network of church-related colleges and universities weakens as schools distance themselves from denominational identification. News coverage of religion is constricted while entertainment media have replaced stock treatment of religious themes and characters with dismissive characterizations of Christianity and fascination with the occult. More telling than the sum of specific indicators, however, is the dramatic shift in public attitudes toward Christianity and its churches. Simply put, the Christian church is no longer conspicuous in American consciousness or integral to American culture.[9]

Given this loss of social position, we need to reconsider how Christian communities might be more faithful in fostering ways of participation in the divine mission of self-giving love and life we confess in Jesus Christ.

8. Of course, the Christian churches, constituting less than 1 percent of the population, have never been at the enter of social or cultural life in Japan.

9. Small, "Changing Times," 3.

Furthermore, a serious reconsideration of educational ministries will require a shift in the way we think about the relation among our natural endowments of perception, action, and cognition. As a consequence of the advent of the research university in the early nineteenth century, the modern period has benefited greatly from analytic modes of thinking, which break up subjects into their component parts or constituent elements. But the modernist analytic rationality brought with it its own inherent problems.

A year following World War I, W. B. Yeats penned his much-quoted poem "The Second Coming,"[10] which depicts the apocalyptic breakdown toward which the West seemed to be rushing headlong. The brutality of "the war to end all wars" had shocked the world into the recognition that the shadow side of modernity had arrived with unimaginable, godless fury. Yeats's poem evokes the kind of post-Babel world we touched on above, where the former common language of Western Christendom had been irreparably confused. In some sense, "The Second Coming" anticipated what postmodernists refer to as *the death of the grand narrative*, which itself has arguably become an alternative grand narrative in the postmodern and post-Christian West. Yeats sees the present moment spinning into the vortex of a violent denouement where a shared past can no longer be relied on and where the future is shrouded by ominous threat, risk, and fear.

> Turning and turning in the widening gyre
> The falcon cannot hear the falconer;
> Things fall apart; the centre cannot hold;
> Mere anarchy is loosed upon the world,
> The blood-dimmed tide is loosed, and everywhere
> The ceremony of innocence is drowned;
> The best lack all conviction, while the worst
> Are full of passionate intensity.

In an eerie premonition of the horrors that haunted much of the rest of the twentieth century, Yeats portrays the basic problem

10. Yeats, "Second Coming," 187.

as an irreparable breach in meaningful communication ("The falcon cannot hear the falconer"). For Yeats, the romantic, the breach between falcon and falconer symbolizes the loss of the instinctive, intuitive relationality that characterized close-knit, premodern societies. This centerless world teeter-totters on the brink of apocalyptic upheaval. With the old world in ruins, a new, anomic world is about to break in like a flood. For Yeats, that new world was not just modernity as the philosophical inheritance of the Enlightenment, but a brutal modernity ushered in by rapid advances in technology and a loss of shared cultural values and identities.[11] Following the global traumas of World War I and the influenza pandemic of 1918, Yeats points to a binary between moral and intellectual ennui ("the best lack all conviction") and the emergence and spread of irrational fanaticism ("the worst are full of passionate intensity").[12]

Here, indifference and fanaticism are paradigmatic and parallel responses to the inbreaking of a totally new future. Out of the chaos of this centerless moment, Yeats conjures up a haunting twist on the ancient Christian creed that proclaims, "He will come again in glory to judge the living and the dead."

> Surely some revelation is at hand;
> Surely the Second Coming is at hand.
> The Second Coming! Hardly are those words out
> When a vast image out of Spiritus Mundi
> Troubles my sight: somewhere in sands of the desert
> A shape with lion body and the head of a man,
> A gaze blank and pitiless as the sun,
> Is moving its slow thighs, while all about it

11. As a historical irony, it should not be forgotten that Yeats was a leader of the so-called Irish Renaissance, which inspired Irish nationalism and the bloody Easter Rebellion of 1916, which won Ireland's independence from Great Britain.

12. Fascism was on the rise globally after World War I, but in the wake of the Second World War, the level of tacit support it received in many countries, including the United States, is easily forgotten. See Paxton, *Anatomy of Fascism*.

> Reel shadows of the indignant desert birds.

Instead of bringing the promised liberation and gracious judgment of the crucified and risen Lord, this antiparousia ushers in a monstrous oppression, symbolized by a slouching beast.

> The darkness drops again; but now I know
> That twenty centuries of stony sleep
> Were vexed to nightmare by a rocking cradle,
> And what rough beast, its hour come round at last,
> Slouches toward Bethlehem to be born?

Before casually rejecting the frightening antiparousia of Yeats's poem, I suggest we allow his vision to haunt us for a moment.

From the vantage point of the Protestant churches today, the Yeats poem may be read as an expression of our fragmentation into the subjectivist, activist, and objectivist factions mentioned above. Yeats's falcon spinning wildly out of the earshot of the falconer is a fitting metaphor for churches and Christians who no longer can hear the Word of God in Jesus Christ in *worship*, bear *witness* to the Word of God in love for neighbors beyond the walls of our particular faith communities, or probe in *wonder* about the Word of God with trusted friends in the community of faith. Plagued by either too much certainty or, conversely, too much doubt, we see everywhere the loss of what Lesslie Newbigin calls a proper Christian confidence, a confidence open to serious interrogation and new insight.[13]

* * *

Whether we belong to churches that emphasize *subjective* religious experience, *active* sociopolitical engagement, *objective* biblical or doctrinal knowledge, or some combination of all three, we "lack all conviction" when we carelessly ignore aspects of the Gospel not suited to our particular faith style. This happens, for example, when we dissect Scripture, searching for some privileged "canon

13. See Newbigin, *Proper Confidence*.

within the canon" that agrees with our particular politics, left or right. In terms of how faith styles relate to the genres of the New Testament, some privilege the teachings of Jesus, others the ethical imperatives of the Gospel, and still others Paul's preaching of the cross and resurrection. Further, we are "full of passionate intensity" whenever we presume ourselves to be the only true inheritors or faithful interpreters of the Gospel. Commenting on the problem of religious intolerance, Benjamin Franklin aptly wrote, "A man must have a good deal of vanity who believes, and a good deal of boldness who affirms, that all the doctrines he holds are true, and all he rejects are false."[14] Today, uncompromising and aggressive sectarian views may be seen, not only in the varieties of religious hucksterism that seduce, frighten, or confuse the credulous, but also in liberal, progressive, or orthodox churches.

Religious indifference and religious fanaticism are both ways of standing in judgment of the word of God in Jesus Christ, granting Christians a wholesale interpretive or ethical freedom, on the one hand, or a fixed interpretive framework and smug sense of moral superiority, on the other. And though we may be tempted to see liberalism and progressivism as modernist, and orthodoxy and some forms of evangelicalism as premodernist, any one of these faith styles, if hardened, may fall prey to the absolutizing tendency of modernity. Whether such a tendency appears in the churches under the guise of subjectivism, activism, or objectivism, the freedom to love God and neighbor will be undermined, and participation in the mission of God harmed. Theology becomes a language game or a political ideology, and spirituality devolves into solipsism or socialization.

As pointed out above, Christian educational ministries have certainly benefited from the advances of modern theories of human development, learning theory, enculturation, multiple intelligences, and so forth. However, as analytic modes replaced synthetic modes of thinking with the rise of modern science, humanities such as theology have become increasingly specialized.

14. Franklin, "Defense of Religious Tolerance," in Isaacson, *Ben Franklin Reader*, 119.

Take New Testament scholarship as one example. There you will find synoptic specialists on Matthew, Mark, or Luke, as well as Johannine specialists, Pauline or sub-Pauline specialists, Apocalyptic specialists, and more. Now, imagine a conversation between one of these specialists and a church historian, systematic theologian, preacher, teacher, or worship leader, and I think you understand my point. Like subjectivist, activist, and objectivist churches and their leaders, when scholars in biblical, historical, systematic/dogmatic, and practical fields are able to understand others only in their professional guilds and are free to pursue careers without connecting to lived communities of faith, there can be little doubt that overspecialization in theology has also contributed to the loss of integration in worship, witness, and wonder.

As a response to this problem, I suggest that we need to draw on more synthetic modes of thinking that focus on the entirety of a particular subject under investigation, rather than only on its constitutive elements. Thus, without rejecting analytic modes of thinking, I will be taking a more synthetic approach to fostering growth in love for God and neighbor in faith communities called to participate in the mission of God in Jesus Christ.

So, how might we begin to approach integrating Christian worship, witness, and wonder? In conversation with postcritical philosopher Michael Polanyi, T. F. Torrance has suggested a helpful, albeit somewhat opaque, approach to this vital question. In *The Mediation of Christ*, Torrance speaks about inquiries in science and theology.

> We develop a form of inquiry in which we allow some field of reality to disclose itself to us in the complex of its internal relations or its latent structure, and thus seek to understand it in the light of its own intrinsic intelligibility or logos. As we do that we come up with a significant clue in the light of which all evidence is then reexamined and reinterpreted and found to fall into a coherent pattern of order. Thus we seek to understand something, not by schematizing it to an external or alien framework of thought, but by operating with a framework of thought appropriate to it, one which it

> suggests to us out of its inherent constitutive relations and which we are rationally constrained to adopt in faithful understanding and interpretation of it.[15]

Let me try to unpack Torrance's dense language and consider how it relates to the problem I have been describing.

Torrance's claim implies that we will never be able to adequately grasp what is really at stake in a field such as practical theology as long as we seek to approach it primarily "from the outside," via the "alien framework" of non-theological academic disciplines. As examples of such "outside-in" approaches, we could point to leading theorists of Christian education variously attempting to describe educational ministry in categories borrowed from theories of cognitive or moral development, socialization, enculturation, existential meaning, self-realization, praxis, critical reflection, theory-laden religious practices, and so forth.[16] Again, without denying a legitimate moment in practical theology for a mutually illuminating conversation with social science or philosophy, I think Torrance rightly makes us suspicious of beginning and ending with such an "outside-in" approach.

To clarify his point with an absurd analogy from medical science, no neuroscientist in his or her right mind would ever dream of trying to understand neurons by first examining liver cells and then applying the conclusions to brain cells. But this kind of schematization "to an external or alien framework of thought" is exactly what happens when practical theologians, often uncritically, make wholesale application of ideas from non-theological disciplines to practical theology. I suggest that this is the kind of well-intentioned but faulty thinking that has contributed to the multiplication of approaches to educational ministry and spiritual growth. The above-mentioned subjectivist, activist, and objectivist orientations both result from and further exacerbate this basic epistemological error. To return to the absurd example from science, instead of moving "outside-in" from liver cells to neurons, a neuroscientist will concentrate his or her full attention and energy

15. Torrance, *Mediation of Christ*, 3–4.

16. See Seymour, *Contemporary Approaches to Christian Education*.

on the painstaking and patient investigation of brain cells. If in the course of the research it turns out that there are similarities discovered between brain cells and cells in other organs, these correspondences would be duly noted.

Similarly, if we are going to take seriously the calling to nurture love for God and neighbor, we should begin with Jesus Christ clothed in his Gospel as the true north to which the community of faith is forever turning. For Christian faith, it is the Son of God—not someone else—who matchlessly embodies love for God and neighbor. He is the One who both lives out and points to the two greatest commandments:

> One of the scribes came near and heard them disputing with one another, and seeing that he answered them well, he asked him, "Which commandment is the first of all?"
>
> Jesus answered, "The first is, 'Hear, O Israel: the Lord our God, the Lord is one; you shall love the Lord your God with all your heart, and with all your soul, and with all your mind, and with all your strength.' The second is this, 'You shall love your neighbor as yourself.' There is no other commandment greater than these." (Mark 12:28–31)

This word of Jesus, which he embodies, enacts, and perfects in his own person and act, takes us back again to the irreducibly theological dimension of our task. If we hope to find some way beyond the muddle in our field, we must overcome our reticence to speak of divine action or agency.[17] So, how is the triune God we confess involved in promoting Christian participation in the mission of God? In the preface to *Theological Science*, Torrance addresses the question of how we might begin such a seemingly daunting inquiry.

> A. E. Taylor called for the locating of authority, neither in individualism nor in some institutional seat, but in a reality which is wholly given and trans-subjective, and simply and absolutely authoritative in its givenness. If

17. See Hastings, *Practical Theology and the One Body of Christ*. In chapter 1, I address this critical lacuna in some leading contemporary models of practical theology.

> knowledge is to be more than personal opinion, he argued, there must be control of our personal intellectual constructions by something which is not constructed but received. In our human knowledge of God this is humbly to acknowledge that what is genuinely given has unquestionable right to control our thinking and acting, just because it is so utterly given to us and not made by us.[18]

When viewed from the standpoint of the "givenness" of divine self-revelation in the incarnation, faith "in Christ"—or more appropriately, the faith "of Christ," which all of the churches continue to confess—cannot be deconstructed into the mutually exclusive orientations of subjectivism, activism, or objectivism without undermining the integrity of the full humanity of the Subject of Christian faith, Jesus Christ himself. Rather, the faith "of Jesus Christ," both within the "triune mystery" of Father, Son, and Holy Spirit and "among us," guides Christians toward a fundamental harmony, "in Christ," between human modes of perception, action, and reflection.

The hardened ideological rivalry between the subjective, activist, and objectivist faith styles and instantiations of the Christian tradition are, *de jure*, overcome in Christ's life-giving, salvific mission from the Father and in the power of the Holy Spirit. From the perspective of an "a posteriori theological realism,"[19] Christian faith, having been embodied by the Son of God under the human conditions of space and time, necessarily embraces every human capacity (subjective or affective, activist or volitional, and objective or cognitive) within a dynamic relational unity. This holistic integration "in Christ" of all aspects of human being is a gracious gift of God's self-revelation in the incarnation. In plain terms, human beings, who by nature and by nurture are not whole, are made whole by the Son of God. Or as the Apostle Paul speaks of this blessed exchange, "For you know the generous act of our Lord Jesus Christ, that though he was rich, yet for your sakes he became poor, so that by his poverty you might become rich" (2 Cor 8:9).

18. Torrance, *Theological Science*, viii.

19. See Hunsinger, *Disruptive Grace*, 210–25.

In the 1970s, the Christian educator John Westerhoff asked whether or not our children would have faith.[20] If my reading of the situation is accurate, the pressing question for the Protestant churches today is whether that faith will be a retreat into a subjectivist, activist, or objectivist silo or whether it will be the faith of Jesus Christ in his fullness as "the Word made flesh," God in the actuality of our full humanity, a faith that unifies and transforms all of the faculties of human beings by the Holy Spirit, who has been poured out on all. For formation in Christian faith to be faithful to the communion shared by Father, Son, and Holy Spirit, a communion whose benefits have been graciously extended to us through the incarnation, we educators of the church must submit ourselves, our theories, and our practices to the God-man Jesus Christ, the incarnate Word of God.

Therefore, just as a brain researcher will focus his or her passionate gaze on brain cells, a practical theologian in the field of Christian educational ministries must carefully and patiently examine how communities of faith participate in the mission of God by fostering growth in the direction of the self-giving love of God and neighbor. The key question for us is, "How do communities of faith promote participation in Jesus Christ and his mission?" As with fruitful research in any other field, new light will be shed on the core problematic of Christian educational ministries only by asking how human beings are turned again and again to love God and neighbor. This is what Torrance means by allowing the field under investigation to disclose to us "its own intrinsic intelligibility or logos."

It should be obvious by now that I will not be suggesting a new paradigm for educational ministry based on some recent development in philosophy or social science. Rather, the admittedly more ambitious goal I have in mind is to argue for the need for a more holistic and integrated theory for Christian educational ministry resonant with the Gospel and the experience of the "holy, catholic, and apostolic church" in its infinitely diverse historical and cultural instantiations.

20. Westerhoff, *Will Our Children Have Faith?*

Without discounting other proximate goals, such as belonging, spiritual enrichment, increasing one's knowledge of Scripture and of theology, or engagement in contemporary issues of peace and justice, I suggest that *participation in the mission of God in Jesus Christ, characterized by growth in love for God and neighbor, is the primary vocation, motivation, and goal of Christian educational ministries and spiritual formation.*

In faithfulness to this primary vocation, motivation, and goal, Christian educational ministries in congregations, families, schools, and other settings will seek creative and relevant ways to integrate three distinctive and complementary modalities into their educational practice. I have chosen the terms *worshiping*, *witnessing*, and *wondering* to identify these three distinctive yet complementary modalities that foster participation in the mission of God in Jesus Christ and in the power of the Holy Spirit. In what follows, I will describe how I came to this understanding. I believe that my tentative conclusions are substantiated by the experience of Israel, the early churches, and faith communities who have pursued educational ministries throughout the ages. As a case study of how the faith surrounding a first-century Palestinian Jew was translated into the thought-and-life worlds of Greco-Roman cultures, we will look in some detail at the ways the Gospel was received and handed on in the post-New Testament churches until the fourth century.

The crisis attending Protestant educational ministries is too serious to limit the audience of this book to peers in the guild of professional practical theologians, though I hope they too will read it. Besides scholars, I hope to also address clergy and laypersons who, by participating in some form of Christian educational ministry as learner or teacher, have wondered what is at stake in the vocation of receiving and handing on the Gospel to others, whether they be the church's children, youth, adults, or converts to Christian faith from other or no religious tradition. While I will treat complex issues, I will try to present these issues in language accessible to the widest possible audience. I will leave it to others to judge whether I have shed some light or only added to the confusion.

2

The Biblical Basis of Christian Worship, Witness, and Wonder

Reflective practitioners of educational ministries soon learn that this vocation is fraught with possibilities and perils both for teachers and for learners. In the words of the Apostle Paul, those of us who "carry this precious Message around in the unadorned clay pots of our ordinary lives" (2 Cor 4:7 MSG) wonder how on earth we might receive and pass on the Gospel in ways that faithfully reflect the grace, beauty, and truth of the God of life and love who comes to us in Jesus Christ and enables participation in God's mission through the power of the Spirit.

In any subject, the disposition of the teacher is critical to successful educational outcomes, and disposition is always shaped by the depth of passionate engagement with the subject matter. Inevitably, teachers in the church will find themselves wrestling Jacob-like with the Subject of the Gospel. As T. F. Torrance points out in his classic introduction to Reformed catechesis, those who receive and those who hand on the Gospel find themselves in the presence of another Teacher, standing on level ground with learners, who share their continual need for confession and forgiveness. "When we encounter the Truth in Christ, we discover that we are at variance with the Truth, in a state of rebellion and enmity toward it, so that the way of knowledge is the way of surrender and acknowledgment through self-denial and repentance."[1]

1. Torrance, *School of Faith*, xxxv.

As I said earlier, when it comes to the Gospel, we are always beginning at the beginning because, regardless of how long we have believed, we can never master the Gospel as we might be able to master quantum mechanics or invertebrate biology. Rather, it is the Subject of the Gospel, the One to whom Scripture testifies, who "masters" us over and over again, through the agency of the Holy Spirit, over the course of a lifetime. The Subject of the Gospel forms, reforms, and transforms a people who are marked by God's self-giving love in baptism by signs of cross and empty tomb.

We have all experienced those moments when a church school class, Bible study, prayer meeting, or new members' class is suddenly transformed into a sacred space and time. Such moments are unpredictable, and they may be accompanied by rejoicing, lament, silence, intense theological debate, confession, forgiveness, song, tears, doxology, prayer, reconciliation, or laughter. Besides such moments of grace, we also experience the deep frustrations and limitations of the educational setting, when there is just not enough time for discussion, when we seem closed off to God's presence and to each other, when we become argumentative or judgmental, when one participant dominates the discussion, or when we as teachers or learners come to our tasks ill prepared. This book is for those who have known such moments and who still see educational ministries as a sacred calling for faith communities today.

On another level, this book is also intended for anyone who has ever marveled how a faith with roots in a first-century society bordering the Mediterranean Sea has managed to be received and transmitted across so many generations and cultural barriers. It is easy to overlook that this long process of reception and transmission has been supported by a range of educational theories and practices in each place and time. But as Walter Brueggemann has pointed out so eloquently, education is a *sine qua non* for the survival of any vital community.

> Every community that wants to last beyond a single generation must concern itself with education. Education has to do with the maintenance of a community through the

> generations. This maintenance must assure enough continuity of vision, value and perception so that the community sustains its self-identity. At the same time, such maintenance must assure enough freedom and novelty so that the community can survive in and be pertinent to new circumstances. Thus, education must attend both to processes of continuity and discontinuity in order to avoid fossilizing into irrelevance on the one hand, and relativizing into disappearance on the other hand.[2]

Within Christian history, as well as reaching back into the history of the people of Israel, we find a rich variety of educational theories and practices that have enabled communities of faith to receive and hand on the Gospel in very different times and places. While we inherit the Gospel as a particular story that in one sense never changes, communities of faith in each time and place also need freedom and nerve to hear and tell the "old, old story" in fresh and relevant ways.

While the New Testament provides surprisingly little detail about the actual educational practices of the first Christian communities, there is no doubt that they gave considerable care to the teaching and learning of the new faith and drew on both Jewish rabbinical and classical Greco-Roman educational models.[3] For example, Paul's letters, which include pastoral admonitions about worship, practical ethical guidelines for living "in Christ," and biblical interpretation and doctrinal material, reflect both the Jewish and the Hellenistic educational views of his time.[4]

In the following key text, Paul recounts the core message of the Gospel (Jesus Christ's salvific death and rising from the dead according to the Scriptures). He uses the Greek pedagogical term *paredōka* to describe the action of "handing down, passing on, transmitting, relating or teaching" the Gospel, and the

2. Brueggemann, *Creative Word*, 1.

3. See Marrou, *History of Education in Antiquity*, 314–29.

4. For those seeking an in-depth analysis of how Paul understood educational ministry, see Osmer, *Teaching Ministry of Congregations*.

term *parelabon* to describe the action of "receiving, accepting, or acknowledging" the Gospel.[5]

> For I *handed on* [*paredōka*] to you as of first importance what I in turn had *received* [*parelabon*]. (1 Cor 15:3a)

For Paul, "handing on" the Gospel is predicated on his having first "received" it, and his letters amply testify that receiving the Gospel involves more than simply hearing and giving intellectual assent.

Elsewhere Paul speaks of this reception using the baptismal metaphor of having been "clothed with" or having "put on" Jesus Christ (Rom 13:14; Gal 3:27). For Paul, receiving the Gospel means participating in Christ, being joined by divine agency to the corporate person Jesus Christ, who continues to be present to his earthly body, the church. In 1 Cor 12:3 Paul speaks of being enabled "by the Spirit of God" to confess "Jesus is Lord." Those who are "in Christ" are graced with an ontological reorientation that Paul elsewhere describes as a "new creation" (2 Cor 5:17; Gal 6:15). While "handing on" the Gospel also embraces the ordinary pedagogical actions of socialization and enculturation, these human actions are all understood to be predicated on the divine agency and grace to which Paul refers by his use of the word "received."

The phrase "receiving and handing on the Gospel of Jesus Christ" conveys the dynamic nature of the process in a way that overcomes the opposition between "socialization" and "transformation," while explicitly naming the content of what faithful Christian communities are called to pass on—namely, the *evangel*, or "Good News," of Christ's self-giving love for God and neighbor. Following Paul, the unique character of the Gospel itself should guide the church's educational ministries from start to finish.

Paul believed that God's Spirit empowers the preaching and teaching of the Gospel.[6] That is, it is the Holy Spirit who confers on believers the benefits of being "in Christ" and who continually

5. See Bauer, *Greek-English Lexicon*, 614–15, 619.

6. See, for example, 1 Cor 3:6–16, where Paul emphasizes the agency of the Spirit in searching the human heart and enabling the knowledge and wisdom of God.

transforms the ancient tradition into a living reality for communities of faith in different times and places. When seen from this perspective, participation in educational ministries is a call to participate in the divine-human drama of redemptive transformation, and our classrooms, retreat centers, or living rooms become sacred spaces where God is present and the community's best pedagogical theories and practices are pressed into service to the gracious Subject of the Gospel. *Christian educational ministries worthy of the name are those empowered by the Holy Spirit.*[7]

Furthermore, in light of Paul's view of the rich variety of spiritual gifts, we may say that, though educational theories and practices will inevitably vary from time to time and from place to place, "the same Spirit . . . activates all of them" (see 1 Cor 12:4–6). Following Paul, I suggest that we need to reclaim the receiving and handing on of Christ's Gospel as a sacred calling, or in today's language, as a communal spiritual discipline whose performance is within the purview of the participants, but whose ground and ends are always dependent on divine agency. Notice one example of how Paul sees ministry in relation to divine agency:

> What then is Apollos? What is Paul? Servants through whom you came to believe, as the Lord assigned to each. I planted, Apollos watered, but God gave the growth. So neither the one who plants nor the one who waters is anything, but only God who gives the growth. The one who plants and the one who waters have a common purpose, and each will receive wages according to the labor of each. For we are God's servants, working together; you are God's field, God's building. (1 Cor 3:5–9)

At a time when the survival of some Protestant churches is uncertain and so many pragmatic proposals for reversing the decline have been put forward, we would do well to begin by reminding ourselves that receiving and handing on the Gospel is always and

7. See Romans 12 on the relation between *praxis* and *charismata*. Since this basic yet unprovable theological percept is suppressed or ridiculed in some academic circles, it is easy to understand why so many practical theologians turn to philosophy or social science, instead of to Scripture and theology, to anchor their theories.

everywhere contingent upon the operation of divine grace. This view, which positions all of the practices that foster the reception and handing on of the Gospel under the aegis of divine gift—which also means that we are in a very real sense never "in charge"—explodes the horizon of hope and imagination as we consider what is really at stake in Christian educational ministries.[8]

At this juncture, I want to return briefly to the Japanese situation because this intercultural, ecumenical perspective may help shed some light on the crisis in our field. While there are many English books that have been written on Christian education, it is telling that the last major one to be translated into Japanese is James Smart's *The Teaching Ministry of the Church*. Even Thomas Groome's 1980 *Christian Religious Education*, undoubtedly the most influential book to appear in this field since Smart's 1954 classic, has not been translated and has received surprisingly little attention.

To my surprise and delight, I found Old Testament scholar Walter Brueggemann's *Creative Word: Canon as a Model for Biblical Education* to be the most helpful book for addressing the problematic of educational ministries in the Japanese churches. The most obvious reason for this preference for Brueggemann over Groome is that Brueggemann's book is more explicitly biblical. Groome's wonderful book, which draws heavily on Aristotle's view of *phronēsis*, critical theory, and theories of human development, assumes a background in culturally specific (i.e., Western) perspectives that sounded alien to my Japanese students. The Japanese Protestant churches are focused on the Bible, which they have in a variety of translations, but they do not necessarily have Aristotle, Habermas, or Piaget for background. Brueggemann's book creatively explores some of the key educational issues that confronted the communities in front of the Old Testament canon. While referring to Scripture and church teaching as "Christian Story," Groome's proposal for "shared praxis" offers surprisingly little

8. While I address the educational ministries of the churches in this book, much of what I propose will also be relevant to other practical theological actions such as preaching, caring, and evangelizing.

guidance about the function of Scripture in educational ministries. In Japan, where the churches represent a tiny minority within a society that self-identifies as Shinto and Buddhist, Christian educational theory and practice cannot evade the primary question of how to sponsor more faithful, culturally situated, contemporary readings of Scripture. Therefore, though Groome's theory was broadly read in the cultural context of North America, Japanese Christians are skeptical of any Christian educational theory or practice that does not first consider how contemporary communities of faith might live more faithfully in the light of the church's canonical writings and doctrinal reflection. I took these concerns of my students seriously and chose Brueggemann over Groome. In the process, I discovered a sound and nuanced biblical basis for the approach to *worship, witness,* and *wonder* that I am presenting in this book.

I turn now in more detail to the relevance of Brueggemann's *Creative Word* for Christian educational ministry today.[9] In conversation with the postcritical biblical approaches of various "canonical critics," Brueggemann focuses on the questions of the final "shape" (Brevard Childs's concern) and the "process" (James Sanders's concern) of the canon in Israel and discerns three ways of knowing: the *ethos* of Torah, the *pathos* of the Prophets, and the *logos* of the Writings. Brueggemann sees the unique function of these three canonical modalities as follows:

The *ethos* of Torah: *What does Israel know about God?* Torah is the "nonnegotiable" and "subversive consensus" that binds together all of the generations of Israel into one people of God. This "predoubt" dimension of the canon has a once-and-for-all quality, since it is the bedrock of the community's identity. Torah is not something each generation needs to reinvent; rather, it is received, pondered, and lived into with gratitude as a sacred gift that has been decisively disclosed. Brueggemann says, "The *ethos* of our community knows that the memory of the stones is

9. Since I can give only a brief synopsis here, I strongly urge readers to read Brueggemann's book, which is a mine of biblical, theological, and pastoral wisdom for the church's lay and ordained educators.

given,[10] settled, and can be trusted. We embrace the *consensus of the Torah*. We have a *disclosure* of God's purpose for and way with his people. That disclosure is sure and undoubted among us."[11] Brueggemann emphasizes that Israel's priests and rabbis wisely discerned that this *ethos* must not be forced upon the community's children. Rather, it is first and foremost embodied by the adults of the faith community and is regularly re-presented in the company of children through ritual, witness, creed, and narrative as a "precious and satisfying" object of wonder.[12]

The *pathos* of the Prophets: *How and where is Israel's identity renewed?* The Prophets deliver a disruptive word on behalf of divine justice, a word that interrogates all settled certainties while reconfirming the divine ground of Israel's faith, hope, and love within the interpretive matrix of sacred history and divine promise. Again and again, prophecy awakens Israel as a bearer of sacred story and witness to eschatological hope. The Prophets sponsor a disquieting renewal under the aegis of the prophetic word that becomes the Word of the Lord. Brueggemann says, "The *pathos* of God leads to a giving of *new truth in uncredentialed channels*. The consensus is shattered by the *disruptive word of the prophet*. In the poetry of *pathos*, the royal definitions of reality are overcome, to end what cannot be ended, to begin what cannot be begun."[13]

In contemporary terms, we might call prophecy the wellspring of the ongoing renewal of Israel's spiritual life. The Prophets are Israel's apostles and preachers.

The *logos* of the Writings: *How should Israel live within the tensions between sacred story, present experience, and eschatological hope?* Brueggemann says that the Writings explore the patterns, paradoxes, and puzzles of divine wisdom and agency in conversation with Israel's lived experience. Here, the kings and sages of Israel try to discern how Israel's sacred story relates to the ethical calling and character of the community today. This dimension of

10. The reference to stones is from Josh 4:21.

11. Brueggemann, *Creative Word*, 91.

12. Brueggemann, *Creative Word*, 16.

13. Brueggemann, *Creative Word*, 91.

the canon promotes both a solemn acknowledgment of the limits of human knowledge and the willingness of the community of faith to take risks on the basis of what has been revealed in Torah and Prophets. Brueggemann says,

> The *logos* of God is the sure ordering of created reality. It is an ordering that requires *wisdom to discern*—an ordering that leads to responsibility and freedom, but also to mystery and awe. The order of life is at times available to us and at times hidden from us. Wisdom is the readiness both to penetrate the mystery and to live obediently with its inscrutability.[14]

The Writings sponsor a process of ethical discernment and risk-taking on behalf of the divine order, even when evidence of the divine presence may be lacking.

Next, I will touch briefly on the harmony or integration between the diverse ways of knowing in Torah, Prophets, and Writings. While Brueggemann devotes a chapter to the particularities of each dimension of the canon, he also affirms that Torah, Prophets, and Writings are inseparable.

> It should be clear that as these elements constitute different pieces of literature, so they also present different intellectual, theological, and educational perspectives. Hopefully, it is equally clear that we are not free to choose one of these to the neglect of others. The juxtaposition of *ethos*, which assures, *pathos*, which wrenches, and *logos*, which instructs, is crucial. The practice of *disclosure*, *disruption*, and *discernment* all are important in faithful living. The life of faith consists in treasuring the consensus, breaking the consensus with new truth, and valuing new experience in tension with the tradition of experience.[15]

To reiterate, the thesis of Brueggemann's book is that *the Old Testament canon embodies three distinct and complementary ways of participation in Israel's sacred story*. For those accustomed to analytic forms of thinking, it is not difficult to grasp the distinctions

14. Brueggemann, *Creative Word*, 91.

15. Brueggemann, *Creative Word*, 91–92.

between the three canonical divisions. But the greater challenge for us lies in holding together the tensions between these distinctive canonical modalities. Here we will need the kind of synthetic imagination to which I referred earlier.

At this juncture, I will insert another biographical word about how Brueggemann's book has inspired my own thinking and teaching. As I introduced seminarians to the wide range of approaches to educational ministry in the history of Christianity, and as I participated in educational ministry in Japanese, international, and US congregations, I became more and more convinced of the need for a unified theory and practice of educational ministries grounded in Scripture and church teaching while critically drawing in an *ad hoc* manner on a variety of traditional and modern approaches.

Reading, teaching, and rereading *The Creative Word* within the intercultural, ecumenical milieu of Japan and the United States led me to wonder whether there might be a similar *ethos-pathos-logos* pattern discernable in the New Testament. I knew from the outset that there were risks involved in this kind of cross-disciplinary search, because, as I mentioned earlier, ever since the nineteenth century, theology has been divided into increasingly autonomous subdisciplines (Bible, history, systematics/dogmatics, and practical). Some of my readers may see such a search as a violation of an academic taboo, because it took me beyond my own field as a practical theologian and intercultural educator.

Eventually, I decided that if an Old Testament scholar like Brueggemann had enough concern for the fractured state of the church's educational ministries to venture into our field of practical theology, I should be willing to tackle themes typically dealt with by biblical studies, albeit from the perspective of an intercultural practical theologian who cares about how Scripture functions within today's communities of faith. So, I wish at the outset to acknowledge my deep debt to Professor Brueggemann, not only for *The Creative Word*, but for the whole corpus of his writings. I see him as an exemplar of the kind of scholar the churches of the Reformation desperately need today, because in spite of his highly regarded academic work, he has never lost sight of congregations as sojourners in faith who live in the real world and yet perceive themselves to be called by the Lord to wrestle with and interpret our sacred texts with hopeful imagination. Having acknowledged this debt, I take full responsibility for the trajectories I propose below from my reading of Brueggemann's work.

I do believe that the educational ministries of the early faith communities in front of the New Testament texts also engaged in a canonical process that echoes yet transforms the *ethos-pathos-logos* pattern Brueggemann so beautifully describes in the communities of Israel in front of the Old Testament texts (see Table 1).

Table 1. Canonical modes of knowing in the Old Testament and New Testament and their echo in ancient catholic church's practices of formation

	Pathos	*Ethos*	*Logos*
Old Testament	Prophets	Torah	Writings
New Testament	*kerygma*	*didachē*	*paraenesis*
Ancient churches	liturgical initiation	baptismal catechesis	moral examination and exhortation

Obviously, in addition to oral and written traditions about Jesus, the Old Testament was sacred Scripture in the earliest Christian communities.[16] The technical term "the law and the prophets," an obvious reference to what would eventually be called the Old Testament, appears several times in the New Testament (Matt 7:12; 22:40; Luke 16:16; Acts 13:15; Rom 3:21). Given this reference to "the law and the prophets" and several hundred direct quotations and indirect allusions, there is no doubt that the Old Testament functioned as the "norm of norms" within which

16. Rather than refer to the "Hebrew Scriptures," I use the traditional designation, not least of all because the earliest Christians used variant cultural forms of the Septuagint (i.e., not in Hebrew but in Greek translation).

the Christ-event was apprehended, interpreted, and proclaimed by the first Christians.

While teaching the history of Christian education, I stumbled onto a correspondence between the Old and New Testament epistemological patterns of *ethos*, *pathos*, and *logos*, not by searching for some "form equivalency" to Torah, Prophets, and Writings within the very different genres of the New Testament, but by thinking about the Japanese church's missional situation in relation to how the Christian churches over the centuries have approached educational ministries. There I kept stumbling on a distinct resonance to the *ethos-pathos-logos* pattern Brueggemann describes in Israel's canon. The brief outline above shows the connections I found between the tripartite canonical modes of knowing in Israel, in the New Testament churches, and in the ancient catholic churches in the Roman Empire.[17]

With some fear and trepidation, I once shared with a renowned New Testament scholar that, based on my reading of Paul's letters and reflection on his missionary journeys, it seems probable that, while New Testament-era apostles, prophets, and evangelists traveled from place to place, teachers or catechists were the first "permanent clergy" to settle down in one place. I added that it is easy to overlook the implicit missiological reason these embryonic communities of faith needed settled leaders; namely, that Gentile converts who had confessed faith in Jesus as the Christ had no knowledge of Israel's Scriptures—the only Bible at the time—so they needed teachers who would commit to the time-intensive work of catechesis.

In time, a "proto-catechumenate" developed that integrated three core aspects of Christian life: (1) regular participation in the community's worship of God and observance of the sacraments, (2) moral teaching and communal ethical discernment about how to live as followers of Jesus, and (3) study of Scripture and confession of faith. Given the missional situation of the earliest

17. I will not touch here on echoes of this tripartite pattern resident in the medieval, Reformation, or modern churches, but I do discuss these briefly in the appendix.

churches as a tiny minority faith, the churches' careful liturgical, ethical, and biblical/theological pedagogy helped Christian faith move beyond its original location in first-century Palestinian Judaism and to take root in new cultural and linguistic settings within and beyond the Roman Empire.

I am happy to report that the New Testament scholar enthusiastically agreed with my inference about the complementary missional collaboration of itinerant preachers and settled teachers and thought it was a good description of what likely happened in the churches that grew out of the Gentile mission. He also admitted that he had never thought about the Jewish-Gentile dynamic in terms of cross-cultural mission, nor had he imagined how catechetical practices were an engine driving the development of church doctrine, theology, and cross-cultural transmission of Christian faith. I concluded by telling my New Testament colleague that, had I not spent twenty years as a missionary working with Japanese pastors, congregations, and theologians, I would never have been alerted to the implicit missional and theological dynamic at work in the communities in front of the New Testament writings. As I mentioned above, while helping prepare Japanese seminarians for congregational ministry, I observed in their churches a missional situation analogous to that of the early churches.

Arising out of Israel's long experience in transmitting a confident and dynamic faith that can bear up under the full weight of human experience, the early Christian churches took pains to carefully nurture adult converts and their children in (1) the *worship* of God in Jesus Christ, who, by the power of the Holy Spirit, continued to be present to the community of faith through proclamation of word and sacrament; (2) the *witness* of a community called to discern how to faithfully love God and neighbor in the face of daunting personal, social, cultural, religious, and political tensions; and (3) through studying and wrestling with Scripture and church teaching, to touch the *wonder* of being part of a community called to participate in the mission of God in Israel and in Jesus Christ.

To repeat, while the genres of the New Testament canon do not, of course, mirror Israel's Torah, Prophets, and Wisdom, we can discern—as a heuristic device—a corresponding substructure in the *didachē* (teaching), *kerygma* (preaching), and *paraenesis* (moral or ethical guidance or advice) interwoven within and across the Gospels, Acts, Letters, and Apocalypse. Under the guidance of the complementary work of itinerant and settled church leaders, the earliest—predominantly Jewish—teachers of the church were completely at home within the tripartite epistemology of Israel's canon, albeit now with a new focus on the crucified and risen Jesus Christ as the One who, in the Spirit poured out "upon all flesh" (Acts 2:17), had extended the gracious promises of Yahweh to all peoples. To conclude this chapter, I have correlated Brueggemann's categories of *pathos*, *logos*, and *ethos* with *worship*, *witness*, and *wonder* in the form of three questions and answers:

1. *The **pathos/worship** question:* If the divine ***pathos*** is communicated by prophets who proclaim the Word of the Lord in Israel, how and where is Christian love for God nurtured and renewed?

   Answer: In a **worshiping** community of faith, Christians learn over a lifetime to love God through an unsettling and liberating process of repentance and forgiveness engendered by the preaching of the Gospel and participation in the sacraments. In Christian worship, the focus is on Jesus Christ, the Word of God, in his office as prophet.

2. *The **logos/witness** question:* If Israel's Writings offer a ***logos*** of accumulated communal wisdom about how to negotiate and renegotiate the tensions between sacred story, present experience, and eschatological promise, how and where is Christian love and care for neighbors in and beyond the faith community nurtured and renewed?

   Answer: In the face of ever-changing personal, social, cultural, religious, and political realities, Christians discern together how best to love and care for their neighbors, thereby giving

witness to Jesus Christ as participants in God's mission in the world. In Christian witness, the focus is on Jesus Christ, the Word of God, in his office as sage-king.

3. *The **ethos/wonder** question:* If the core ***ethos*** in Israel is mediated by its identity given in Torah, how and where does the Christian community learn its identity in relation to God and neighbor?

   Answer: In intentional educational settings marked by practices of **wondering**, Christian communities grow in their understanding of the Gospel of Jesus Christ by studying and interrogating Scripture and church teaching.[18] Here, the focus is on Jesus Christ, the Word of God, in his office as priest.[19]

* * *

Please note the deliberate change in order here and the correlation with a Reformed understanding of the *munus triplex* ("threefold office") of Jesus Christ as Prophet, Priest, and King. In my view,

18. If Torah provides the basis for knowledge of God, confession of faith, and religious identity in Israel, and if the story of Israel and the church's interpretation of Jesus Christ provide the basis for the knowledge of God, confession of faith, and religious identity in the Christian community, I have decided to use the New Testament term "Gospel" as the closest Christian analogue to Torah, referring in the broadest sense to the tradition of the "Good News of or about Jesus Christ" and not exclusively to "Gospels" (as in the "Four Gospels"), the Pauline or deutero-Pauline "Gospel" of the Epistles, or the apocalyptic "Gospels" found in Revelation or other New Testament writings. Just as the Torah encompasses the inexhaustibly rich strands of the biblical narrative and intracanonical traditions of theological interpretation in Israel, so the Gospel similarly encompasses the stories of Jesus and the core confession of Jesus as the Christ within the communities of faith in front of the diverse writings of the New Testament and, by implication, within Christian communities of faith in all times and places.

19. The use of the word "ethical" or "ethic" here should not be confused with our prior use of the word *ethos*. When I refer to the *ethos* of the Torah or the Gospel, I mean "the characteristic spirit of the Jewish or Christian culture or community as manifested in its specific story, beliefs, and aspirations." When I mention "ethical," I mean "of or relating to the moral principles of a particular faith."

the *worship-witness-wonder* paradigm I am proposing reflects the New Testament's continuity with and transformation of the Old Testament paradigm. Here we begin not with the Torah, as in Israel, but with the divine-human encounter of the Christ-event, or the Word of God in Jesus Christ, where that event or word is prophesied/preached/proclaimed. The encounter with Jesus Christ as Word of God motivated early missionary witnesses like Paul to proclaim Good News *both within and beyond* the synagogue, "to the Jew first and also to the Greek" (Rom 1:16). The third dimension, *wonder*, which builds on the encounter with the Word in *worship* and *witness* to the Word in the world, refers to those sites where Christian confession, doctrine, theology, and devotion gradually take shape within each new social, cultural, and political setting. Whether we think, for example, of the calling of the disciples, the commissioning of the Samaritan woman at the well, Pentecost, or Paul's conversion, the divine-human encounter with the Word (*worship*) inspires a community to bear that Word into all spheres of life (*witness*), which in turn inspires the community's studied and imaginative reflection in light of the Word in Israel's Scripture and in Jesus Christ (*wonder*).

In the following three chapters, we will survey the pattern of *pathos and worship, logos and witness*, and *ethos and wonder* implicit in the ancient church's baptismal catechesis, while touching on some implications for churches today. Beginning with Vatican II and the subsequent liturgical renewal that profoundly influenced many churches, both Protestant and Roman Catholic, there has been a steady interest in the prebaptismal catechetical and liturgical practices of the early churches. When we read the primary sources, we are impressed by the apparent degree of devotion to Jesus Christ, obedience to the church's ethical and moral teachings, and knowledge of Scripture and church teaching.

Frustrated by the sense of the church's accommodation with contemporary culture, we can be tempted to romanticize the early Christians. Some churches have revived some of the more arcane practices of the ancient churches (e.g., baptismal exorcism and chrismation). However, as we consider formation for participation in the mission of God today against the background of the practices of the ancient churches, I think we should avoid jumping too quickly to any conclusions about any retrieval of practices. Indeed, though there is much to learn from the ancient churches, we also need to take seriously our own missional contexts. Rather than dusting off exotic ancient practices, overcoming the lamentable divisions in the Protestant churches, which I have described in chapter 1, will call for prayerful, creative, and thoughtful engagement.

3

Pathos and Christian Worship: Renewal in Word and Sacrament for Participation in God's Mission

*The **pathos/worship** question:* If the divine ***pathos*** is communicated by prophets who proclaim the Word of the Lord in Israel, how and where is Christian love for God nurtured and renewed?

Answer: In a **worshiping** community of faith, Christians learn over a lifetime to love God through an unsettling and liberating process of repentance and forgiveness engendered by the preaching of the Gospel and participation in the sacraments. In Christian worship, the focus is on Jesus Christ, the Word of God, in his office as prophet.

IN *THE EARLY CHURCH*, Henry Chadwick attributes the high degree of unity achieved by the first churches to "a common faith and a common way of ordering their life and worship. Whatever differences there might be of race, class, or education, they felt bound together by their focus of loyalty to the person and teaching of Jesus."[1] Such loyalty entailed an intimate and personal identification with Jesus, a relation built on regular participation in the worship life of the community of faith and nurtured by the sense of wonder engendered by the preaching and teaching of the Gospel. The worship of the churches focused on the Spirit's

1. Chadwick, *Early Church*, 32.

ongoing witness to the redemption accomplished in the death and resurrection of Jesus Christ and in anticipation of the consummation of all things at the end of the age.

The initiatory sacrament of baptism commemorated Jesus' filling with the Spirit at his own baptism by John. To be identified in baptism with the crucified and risen Lord (see Romans 6) meant a renunciation of evil and a reception of a new life in the power of the Holy Spirit, who continued to make Christ present. Likewise, the recurring sacrament of the Eucharist was "received not as common food for satisfying hunger and thirst, but as the flesh and blood of Christ."[2] Recounting the words of Jesus at the Last Supper, Paul had to remind the careless Corinthians that the Eucharist was to be administered with solemnity "in remembrance" of the Lord's death (1 Cor 11:25).

The centrality of baptism and Eucharist, and the careful initiation of new converts into the pattern of dying and rising with Jesus Christ, reveals the early church's theological conviction that the Spirit who had been poured out on Jesus continued to be poured out upon the church. By the early third century, the baptismal interrogation of the *Apostolic Tradition* includes the question, "Dost thou believe in *the* Holy Spirit *in* the Holy Church?"[3] This wording may suggest that the Holy Spirit, which had been poured out "upon all flesh" at Pentecost, was now understood to be limited to the church. Undoubtedly, this emphasis on the church as the Spirit's exclusive sphere of influence was not unrelated to the minority church's bitter struggle with internal and external challenges to the unity and authority of Christian faith. Cyprian consolidates this defensive apologetic later in the third century, writing, "The Holy Spirit is one, and cannot dwell with those outside the community . . . It follows that there can be no baptism among heretics;

2. Chadwick, *Early Church*, 262.

3. Hippolytus, *Apostolic Tradition*, 37; italics mine. The later Apostles' Creed ("I believe in the Holy Ghost; the holy catholic Church") retains this connection. There are significant textual problems with *The Apostolic Tradition*, but generally scholars agree it was written around 215 and probably reflects practices common to that period (Westerhoff and Edwards, *Faithful Church*, 50).

for baptism is based on this same unity and cannot be separated either from the Church or from the Holy Spirit."[4] Thus, the church was seen as a unique site of formation and transformation, the place where the Holy Spirit communicated the presence, faith, and benefits of the Lord Jesus Christ. Polemics aside, without such a strong faith in the power of the Holy Spirit to transform a person into a Christian—one in Christ who bears Christ's name, belongs to Christ, participates in Christ and his mission of self-giving and redemptive love for the world—the church would probably not have invested so much time and energy into nurturing new converts into its faith and its practices of worship.

While we may not be comfortable with the notion that the Holy Spirit works exclusively in the church, it is striking to note the confidence here that a person could be transformed by the Spirit in the community of faith. Indeed, the promise of transformation by God within a human community may seem a shocking boast to the postmodern mind, but it is precisely the promise the ancient church held out to inquirers.

We turn now to a fourth-century document to unpack some of the other convictions that grounded the church's theological confidence. In his first address to those approved for the eight-week-long prebaptism lectures,[5] Bishop Cyril of Jerusalem speaks with surprising aplomb about a person's motive in seeking baptism.

> Possibly too you have come on another pretext. It is possible that a man is wishing to pay court to a woman, and came hither on that account. The remark applies in like manner to women also in their turn. A slave also perhaps wishes to please his master, and a friend his friend.

4. Cyprian, *Christian Initiation*, in *The Early Christian Fathers*, 269.

5. A series of eighteen lectures delivered during the Lenten season in the church in Jerusalem. After a *procatechesis* (prologue) that introduced candidates to the process they were about to undergo and five introductory lectures on confession, repentance, remission of sins, the adversary, baptism, an exhortation on ten points of doctrine and related ethical issues and a lecture on faith, lectures six through eighteen were devoted to an exposition of the Jerusalem Creed. Five additional lectures called the Mystagogical Lectures were presented after baptism.

> I accept this bait for the hook, and welcome you, though you came with an evil purpose, yet as one to be saved by a good hope. Perhaps you knew not whither you were coming, nor in what kind of net you are taken. You have come within the Church's nets: be taken alive, flee not: for Jesus is angling for you, not in order to kill, but by killing to make alive: for you must die and rise again. For you have heard the Apostle say, *Dead indeed unto sin, but living unto righteousness.* Die to your sins, and live to righteousness, live from this very day.[6]

The church puts out the net, but it is Jesus Christ himself, still present through the Spirit's agency, who "fishes" for the person. Instead of boasting in human agency or authority, the bishop is confident that God's power operates within the church. As a place where the transformational spiritual encounter takes place, the church simply invites the seeker to enter in, to participate and grow in Jesus Christ.

It is important to note that liturgical initiation was not carried out in isolation from careful teaching of church doctrine. As we will see in chapter 5, creeds or confessions of faith, which eventually evolved into declaratory creeds used in public worship, functioned as the "explicit curriculum" in the prebaptismal instruction of catechumens.[7] The solemn presentation, reception, and reiteration of this hallowed summary of the Gospel were key educative or formational moments that accompanied liturgical initiation into the community of faith. In the baptismal interrogation, the bishop confirmed the candidate's mastery of the creed's content and faith in its Subject.

In centering its catechesis on a clearly defined, trustworthy rule of faith, confession, or creed, we might wonder how the early Christians avoided the pitfall of the confessionalism, creedalism, or propositionalism that is a legacy in some "orthodox" Protestant churches today. What were the practical means employed in nurturing a dynamic faith that captured not only the minds but

6. Cyril, *Catechetical Lecture*, 5:2.

7. See Eisner, *Educational Imagination*.

also the passions of new converts? The goal of early catechesis was not the transmission of doctrinal knowledge for its own sake but the holistic conversion of mind, heart, and practice in the light of the Gospel. Thus, even with all of its emphasis on learning the creed, the creed itself was never the goal of Christian formation. Pointing to the divine reality, the creed provoked wonder, contemplation, and imagination. We might say that the ultimate goal of catechesis was *participatio Christi*, a transformation in the direction of a life of faith, hope, and love patterned on, even participating in, Jesus Christ.

Again, the catechesis of the early church was based on the confidence that the Holy Spirit continued, through the worship of the church, to engender discernible and lasting changes in the lives of Christians. Through the teaching of the triune creed, the Christian's life was correlated directly to the life of Jesus as recounted in the apostolic stories of the church and in the communion of love of Son, Father, and Holy Spirit. It is therefore not surprising that the church's teachers showed as much concern for personal transformation as for orthodoxy of faith, believing that the Holy Spirit was effectively present and creating Christian witnesses whose lives would reflect the self-giving love of God in Jesus Christ.

As we explore how the liturgy of the church helped to shape a Christian temperament, we need to consider the relationship between affect and cognition. Reflecting on the initiation process of the early church, John Berntsen says, "Catechesis is the shaping of religious emotions and affections in the context of teaching doctrine."[8] At first glance, Berntsen's conjunction of affect and cognition ("teaching doctrine") may seem novel or even untenable to a modern, analytic mind. Indeed, the modernist epistemology tried very hard to separate "first-order" emotional perception from "second-order" cognitive reflection, and many modern theologians have ascribed wholeheartedly to this separation. One example is Paul Tillich. While offering important insights on the practical theological concern of religious education, Tillich does

8. Berntsen, "Christian Affections and the Catechumenate," 229.

not shed much light on the interrelation between emotion and cognition in actual educational practice.

> The educational function of the church does not consist in information about the history and the doctrinal self-expressions of the church. A confirmation-instruction which does merely misses its purposes, although it may communicate useful knowledge. Neither does the educational function of the church consist in the awakening of a subjective piety, which may be called conversion but which usually disappears with its emotional causation. A religious education which tries to do this is not in line with the educational function of the church. The church's task is to introduce each new generation into the reality of the Spiritual Community, into its faith and into its love. This happens through participation in degrees of maturity, and it happens through interpretation in degrees of understanding. There is no understanding of a church's life without participation; but without understanding the participation becomes mechanical and compulsory.[9]

In support of Tillich, we should remember he was engaged in a struggle to translate the Gospel into a recognizable modern idiom while rejecting the tendency toward individualistic emotional excess, on the one hand, or legalistic scholastic orthodoxy, on the other. Though his language is suggestive, Tillich cannot overcome the modernist divorce of cognition and emotion and offers inspiring words but vague counsel on how the churches might practically nurture the passions, actions, and intellect of each new generation.[10] But *how* is a Christian nurtured into what Tillich calls the "reality of the Spiritual Community"?

Michael Polyani and other philosophers of science have claimed that all forms of human knowing entail self-investment and tacit emotional and fiduciary dimensions. Speaking of the passions of the scientist, Polanyi says,

9. Tillich, *Systematic Theology*, 194.

10. In the more liberal Protestant churches, an overwhelmingly negative view of church doctrine has surely been influenced by Tillich and others.

> From the start of this book I have had occasion, in various contexts, to refer to the overwhelming elation felt by scientists at the moment of discovery, an elation of a kind which only a scientist can feel and which science alone can evoke in him . . . I quoted the famous passage in which Kepler announced the discovery of his Third Law: ". . . nothing holds me; I will indulge my sacred fury . . ." The outbreak of such emotions in the course of discovery is well known, but they are not thought to affect the outcome of discovery. Science is regarded as objectively established in spite of its passionate origins. It should be clear by this time that I dissent from that belief; and I have come to the point at which I want to deal explicitly with passions in science. I want to show that scientific passions are no mere psychological by-product, but have a logical function which contributes an indispensable element to science.[11]

If passion positively contributes to advances in science, should we not also expect passion to make a positive contribution to the spiritual life? With the help of Polanyi, Kuhn, and others, the dualistic epistemology that attempts to bracket out the passions of the subject in human knowing events is being rethought across academic disciplines. The churches should rejoice that the affective or perceptual dimension, so obviously an essential element in religious belief, is at last being given serious reappraisal for its important role in human knowing.

Thus, instead of seeing emotions as purely subjective, irrational, and idiosyncratic, it is possible under an expanded epistemology to claim that religious emotions have a "logic" of their own that may complement cognitive beliefs.[12] Berntsen helps unpacks this positive relation in more detail.

> [Emotions] are not . . . wholly intelligible apart from the thoughts, reasons, beliefs and knowledge that go along with them. Being affected by something presupposes having in some fashion perceived, remembered, believed

11. Polanyi, *Personal Knowing*, 134.

12. Berntsen, "Christian Affections," 232.

> or known it. It is not that, say, the religious person's "fear of the Lord" just *is* a belief or a thought about the divine; but such affective regard for the religious object presupposes who or what the divine is believed, described and thought to be. The appraisal of the divine articulated by a religious teaching, whether it is explicit or not, is part of any description of the emotions involved. Emotion and thought are not different floors of a building but connecting rooms in the same suite . . . To be affected but not about, at or for anything would be odd. The father does not simply rejoice, but rejoices *over* the prodigal or *upon* the occasion of the latter's return.[13]

To return to ancient liturgical formation, the rhetorical teachers of the church sought to rouse the catechumen's emotions in tandem with their growing knowledge of the content of the Gospel, granting priority neither to cognitive reflection nor to affective perception. Emotive religious experience and cognitive doctrine were "not opposed but entailed each other."[14] Emotion and cognition were seen in a complementary relationship. Again, as Berntsen further suggests,

> The shaping of the affections was a fundamental intention of their catechetical strategy. Far from showing they had no vital interest in teaching and doctrine, however, this attests precisely to their concern for the conditions under which teaching and doctrine were received. Second, more than anything else about a candidate's affective state, the early catechists were concerned with its quality. Though they certainly recognized a difference between such things as emotion and thought or intellectual assent and experience, they did not oppose them. They wanted to know what *kind* of dispositions and affections you had, not how these differed from your thoughts and beliefs.[15]

Christian faith was understood not simply as intellectual assent to the creed, but it touched on the deepest emotional needs for

13. Berntsen, "Christian Affections," 232.

14. Berntsen, "Christian Affections," 231.

15. Berntsen, "Christian Affections," 234.

love, acceptance, and belonging. Hence, the emotions were neither suppressed nor overemphasized but were encouraged within the context of corporate worship. Cognitive and emotional wonder attended the proclamation, explication, and hearing of the Christian Scriptures and the administration of the sacraments.

Next, with our primary sources in Cyril's *Catechetical Lectures* (c. 350) and the Diary of Egeria, a Spanish pilgrim who visited Jerusalem around 380, we will consider in more detail how the fourth-century church in Jerusalem nurtured Christian affections and dispositions by immersion in a liturgical process that involved a wide range of ritual acts, including regular participation in the worship of the community, prayer, exorcism, anointing, fasting, and so forth.

The social situation of Christianity changed dramatically under the reign of Emperor Constantine (306–37). Whereas Christians had been accustomed to meeting in houses before Constantine's conversion around 312, suddenly great churches began to be constructed in honor of the apostles and martyrs. Jerusalem became a magnet for pilgrims from all over the Roman Empire. There, Constantine had ordered the construction of the Martyrium, a church commemorating Jesus Christ's crucifixion, and the nearby Anastasis, a smaller shrine commemorating his resurrection. It was to those hallowed shrines that eager candidates for baptism began journeying in the weeks prior to Easter.

By the fourth century, it appears that the length of prebaptismal catechesis had been reduced from the three years mentioned in the *Apostolic Tradition*. In neither Cyril nor Egeria do we find mention of the Jerusalem church requiring prior instruction of those who sought to be enrolled in the eight-week catechesis leading up to baptism at Easter. In addition to being a time for the training and reception of new members, those eight weeks were also becoming a time of repentance and self-examination for the entire community of faith.[16] Osmer says,

16. Osmer, *Confirmation*, 45. The practice of the forty days of Lent also began sometime in the fourth century, and it is likely related to this period of prebaptismal catechesis.

> All baptized members were encouraged to participate vicariously in the intense preparation of catechumens as a way of renewing their own commitment to the faith. They were free to attend the catechetical lectures and to witness the various liturgical events that accompanied the process . . . The first catechetical lecture, the Procatechesis, took place in the presence of the entire congregation, reminding every member of the seriousness of this step.[17]

The dramatic effect that the Jerusalem church's catechesis had on initiates and the congregation cannot be underestimated.[18] Following the first lecture, the catechumens would go to the Martyrium at dawn each morning to be exorcized, one by one, before gathering around the bishop's throne to hear his lectures. Exorcism, presumably a common practice in the early churches, involved the laying on of hands, and it "remained one of the most personal elements of the catechumenate."[19] The exorcist used water, salt, and oil to "cleanse" catechumens every day during the eight weeks prior to Easter.[20] Other physical actions associated with exorcism include the *exsufflatio*, or breathing out of the devil, and the *insufflatio*, or the breathing in of the Holy Spirit.

Though the dualistic worldview common at the time surely accounts in part for this practice, we may also situate exorcism in relation to early Christian biblical interpretation. The allegorical, or "spiritual," method of reading Scripture, wherein Israel's story was seen to prefigure the story of Christ and the church, was common in the ancient church. As we see, for example, in his first "mystagogic lecture" for the newly baptized, Cyril likens Christian baptism to the Passover deliverance of the people of Israel from the bondage of Egypt. Just as Israel had suffered in bondage to Pharaoh until the blood of the Passover lamb was daubed on Israel's doorposts, so the baptismal candidate was thought to be in

17. Osmer, *Confirmation*, 45.

18. Clearly the drama was enhanced by the locale of the Holy City.

19. Osmer, *Confirmation*, 45.

20. Folkemer, "Study of the Catechumenate," 255.

bondage to Satan until Christ shed his blood on the cross. Thus, the crossing of the Red Sea prefigured the salvific action of baptism. Cyril says, "There the tyrant [Pharaoh] was pursuing the ancient people even to the sea; and here, the daring and shameless spirit, the author of evil, was following you even to the very streams of salvation. The tyrant of old was drowned in the sea; and this present one disappears in the water of salvation."[21]

Baptism was understood as a divine action administered in God's name, therefore the regular exorcisms also invoked the divine names. Gifford notes that some early invocations used in exorcisms were "The God of Abraham, and God of Isaac, and God of Jacob," "The God of Israel," and "The God who drowned the king of Egypt and the Egyptians in the Red Sea."[22] Cyril directly links the action of the exorcist with God's action, saying that, because of the power of the Holy Spirit, whom he calls "A mighty ally and protector . . . and great Teacher of the Church," "the mere breathing of the Exorcist becomes as a fire to that unseen foe."[23] These daily exorcisms culminated in final exorcisms by the bishop on Holy Saturday and finally, at the candidate's renunciation of Satan and all of his pomp just prior to stepping into the baptismal pool in the dawn of Easter Sunday. Exorcism, says Folkemer, does not imply that all believers were thought to be "obsessed like demoniacs, but only that in consequence of original sin and of personal sins, they were subject more or less to the power of the devil." Exorcism was seen as a "cleansing formula . . . anticipating the principal effect of baptism."[24]

In addition to daily attendance at the bishop's lectures, catechumens participated in the church's regular service of worship, albeit on a limited basis. Services were divided into two parts: the "liturgy of the catechumens" and the "liturgy of the faithful." The catechumens and other inquirers participated in the first part of

21. Cyril, *Catechetical Lectures*, 19:3.

22. Gifford, "Introduction," in Schaff and Wace, *Nicene and Post-Nicene Fathers*, VII:xix, xx.

23. Cyril, *Catechetical Lectures*, 16:19.

24. Folkemer, "Study of the Catechumenate," 255.

the service, consisting mainly of Scripture readings, exhortations, and a homily. According to A. Cleveland Coxe, the general pattern of the ancient liturgy was preparatory prayers, followed by the reading of psalms, the Acts, or the Epistles, and a Gospel text read by a deacon or presbyter. Coxe continues,

> Then followed an exhortation from one or more of the presbyters; and the bishop or president delivered a homily or sermon, explanatory, it should seem, of the Scripture which had been read, and exciting the people to an imitation of the virtues therein exemplified. When the preacher had concluded his discourse with a doxology in praise of the Holy Trinity, a deacon made a proclamation for all infidels and non-communicants to withdraw; then came the dismissal of several classes of catechumens . . . after the prayers for each respectively.[25]

We see from this description that the hearing of Scripture, exhortations, homilies, and even the dismissal were all solemn liturgical acts in which catechumens participated as part of the initiation into the full worship of the community of faith.[26]

Turning now to Egeria's account, we learn that the bishop's lectures presented baptismal candidates with an outline of the Bible. Equipped with a general outline of salvation history and a creedal summary of the received tradition of faith, those attending the daily lectures must have found these preparatory services to have left a deep emotional and intellectual impression. Speaking to the educational "outcomes" of this approach, in which the apostolic tradition functioned as the interpretive filter for the hearing of Scripture, Egeria adds, "Thus it is that in these places all the faithful are able to follow the Scriptures when they are read

25. Coxe, "Introductory Notice," in Roberts and Donaldson, *Ante-Nicene Fathers*, VII:535.

26. In the wake of the liturgical renewal movement, some contemporary Protestant churches have revived and reinterpreted this part of the ancient rite by offering a prayer or blessing for noncommunicants during communion.

in the churches, because all these are taught through those forty days . . . for three hours."[27]

Baptism was the dramatic climax of the eight-week initiation. After participating in the services of Holy Week along with other pilgrims to Jerusalem, baptismal candidates would gather at the Martyrium on Holy Saturday and spend the day and night praying and fasting in a final Easter vigil. In the early hours before dawn on Sunday, they would at last proceed to the baptistry, which was likely located in the Anastasis, the shrine commemorating the resurrection. There, they would disrobe and be anointed one last time with the oil of exorcism. This was followed by a final renunciation when each candidate would face toward the west, which Cyril calls "the region of sensible darkness," stretch out his or her arms toward Satan "as though he were present," renounce Satan, all his works ("sin" or "deeds and thoughts which are contrary to reason"), and all his pomp ("the madness of theatres, horse races, hunting and all such vanity"). Here is how Cyril interprets the intention of this act of renunciation in the first postbaptismal mystagogic lecture: "What then did each of you stand up and say? 'I renounce you, Satan,' you wicked and most cruel tyrant, meaning, 'I fear your power no longer; because Christ has overthrown your power, having partaken with me of flesh and blood, that through these he might destroy death, that I might not be subject to bondage forever.'"[28]

After this dramatic liturgy, the candidates would be led, one by one, into the baptismal pool and, responding to an interrogative form of the creed, would confess the Trinitarian faith in response to the bishop's questions. After coming up out of the water, each would be anointed with oil again, this time as a sign of the reception of the Holy Spirit, and would be clothed in a white robe. Cyril's description of chrismation on the forehead, ears, nostrils and breast shows how thoroughly—in thought, word, and bodily action—the new Christian was exhorted to identify with Jesus himself.

27. Egeria, *Travels*, 123–24.

28. Cyril, *Catechetical Lectures*, 19:4.

> You were first anointed on the forehead, that you might be delivered from shame, which the first man who sinned carried with him everywhere; and that "with unveiled face you might reflect as a mirror the glory of the Lord" [2 Cor 3:18]. Then on your ears; that you might receive the ears which are quick to hear the Divine Mysteries, of which Isaiah says, "The Lord gave me also an ear to hear" [Isa 50:4]; and the Lord Jesus in the Gospel, "He that has ears to hear let him hear" [Matt 11:15]. Then on the nostrils; that receiving the sacred ointment you may say, "We are to God a sweet savour of Christ, in them that are saved" [2 Cor 2:15]. Afterwards on your breast; that having put on "the breast-plate of righteousness," you may "stand against the wiles of the devil" [Eph 6:14, 11]. For as Christ after his baptism, and the visitation of the Holy Ghost, went forth and defeated the adversary, so likewise you, after Holy Baptism and the Mystical Chrism, having put on the whole armour of the Holy Ghost, are to stand against the power of the adversary and vanquish it, saying, "I can do all things through Christ which strengthens me" [Phil 4:13].[29]

This anointing with oil was charged with profound theological meaning. It was seen as a sacred action that, through the agency of the Holy Spirit, dramatized the believer's identification with and participation in Jesus Christ. In the third postbaptismal mystagogic lecture, Cyril eloquently illustrates the correspondence between the believer's anointing at baptism and Christ's anointing. "As he was anointed with an ideal oil of gladness, that is, with the Holy Ghost . . . so you have been anointed with ointment, having been made partakers and fellows of Christ."[30]

When everyone was thus baptized and anointed, they would process together, carrying lit torches into the Martyrium, where the gathered community of faith was waiting. This dramatic moment, when the newly baptized would be joined to the faithful for full participation in the church's worship, had been foreshadowed again and again throughout the bishop's lectures. We have one

29. Cyril, *Catechetical Lectures*, 21:4.

30. Cyril, *Catechetical Lectures*, 21:2.

such example from Egeria, in which she quotes the bishop's admonition to the candidates after the ceremonial *redditio symboli* (the reciting, or "giving back," the creed), which took place during the final week of instruction.

> During these seven weeks you have been instructed in the whole law of the Scriptures, and you have heard about the faith. You have also heard of the resurrection of the flesh. But as for the whole explanation of the Creed, you have heard only that which you are able to know while you are still catechumens. Because you are still catechumens, you are not able to know those things which belong to a still higher mystery, that of baptism. But that you may not think that anything would be done without explanation, once you have been baptized in the name of God, you will hear of them during the eight days of Easter in the Anastasis following the dismissal from church. Because you are still catechumens, the most secret of the divine mysteries cannot be told to you.[31]

Such admonitions would have certainly intensified the emotions of the candidates. At last, as the Easter morning sun was rising, the newly baptized would partake of the Eucharist for the first time in the company of their new family in Christ. During the following days, they would attend five mystagogic lectures, which focused on the subjects of baptism, chrism, and the liturgy of the Eucharist.

Robin Lane Fox says that early Christian initiation was "not a process dominated, or largely explained, by sudden miracles . . . People felt they were exploring a deep mystery, step by step."[32] As a missional response to the practices of the popular mystery cults of the day, Christian liturgical initiation in the fourth century was a careful process combining teaching of the creed with participation in the sacraments of baptism and Eucharist. The ultimate goal of catechesis was participation in Christ.

Referring to the power of ritual, anthropologist Clifford Geertz says, "Whatever role divine intervention may or may not

31. Egeria, *Travels*, 124–25.

32. Fox, *Pagans and Christians*, 317.

play in the creation of faith . . . it is, primarily at least, out of the context of concrete acts of religious observance that religious conviction emerges on the human plane."[33] Christian educators have long recognized the importance of worship in spiritual formation, but recently more attention has been given to the practical theological question of why worship is so central. From the brief sketch presented here, it should be clear that the ancient church's prebaptismal catechesis was a ritual-laden preparation for holistic participation in the way of Jesus Christ.

If the creed (i.e., church doctrine) is the "explicit curriculum," what is the "implicit curriculum" of liturgical initiation? Jeff Astley says that "what is learned in Christian worship is a range of emotions, experiences and attitudes that lie at the heart of Christian spirituality."[34] At the same time, he reminds us that worship is not simply a means to some other end, educational or otherwise. Astley quotes Geoffrey Wainwright, who says worship is an "explicitly religious form of play." That is, worship is "an end in itself" or a "non-goal directed activity":[35]

> Whatever account of objective religious experience is accepted, the point is that worship may serve to prepare for, allow and evoke experiences of God. It may put people in the place, psychologically and epistemologically, where God can be "seen" and "heard." That would be learning-through-experience with a vengeance.[36]

In combination with ritual actions, language plays a powerful formative role in worship. Astley describes worship language as performing "non-cognitive, rather than cognitive functions. Language used in worship does not directly assert facts or provide descriptions. 'Holy, holy, holy, Lord God of hosts; heaven and earth are filled with your glory' does not serve as a description of

33. Geertz, *Interpretation of Cultures*, 112–13.
34. Astley, "Role of Worship in Christian Learning," 244.
35. Astley, "Role of Worship in Christian Learning," 245.
36. Astley, "Role of Worship in Christian Learning," 249.

God, but as an expression of praise to him."[37] Borrowing Austin's concept of "performatives," that is, "words, phrases or sentences which *do* things (other than make statements), speech acts that make requests or promises or warnings," Astley describes some of the performatives used in worship.[38] It is easy to see how various forms of prayer, confession of sin, creeds, praise, exhortations, renunciations, declarations of forgiveness, benedictions, exorcisms, and so forth used in the ancient liturgy all fit into one or more of these categories of performative speech.

In addition to whatever "vertical effect" such speech acts might have, Astley points to "a more tangible 'horizontal effect . . . in their perlocutionary effect on fellow worshippers and, in a reinforcing way, back onto the language user him/herself. It is this perlocutionary effect of the language of worship that I have described as evoking, sustaining and deepening religious attitudes and religious experiences."[39]

Using Evans's list of "attitude-virtues," Astley enumerates eight affective attitudes that "Christian liturgy, hymnody and liturgical preaching serve to express and evoke": basic trust, humility, self-acceptance, responsibility, self-commitment, friendliness, concern, and contemplation.[40] These are virtues that characterize the Christ-centered *koinōnia* described by Christian ethicist Paul Lehmann as

> a laboratory of maturity in which, by the operative (real) presence of the Messiah-Redeemer in the midst of his people, the will to power is broken and displaced by the power to will what God wills . . . Maturity is the full development in a human being of the power to be

37. Astley, "Role of Worship in Christian Learning," 246.

38. These "include 'verdictives' (evaluative judgments), 'exercitives' (commands, requests, etc.), 'commissives' (promises and expression of intention), and 'behabitives' (expressions of attitude and social behaviour)" (Astley, "Role of Worship in Christian Learning," 246).

39. Astley, "Role of Worship in Christian Learning," 246–47. The "perlocutionary effect" refers to the impact a speech act has on its hearers.

40. Astley, "Role of Worship in Christian Learning," 247–48.

> truly himself in being related to others who have also the power to be truly and fully themselves.[41]

* * *

In this chapter, we have seen that the process of catechesis in the early church, while being centered on a normative confession of faith, was a thoroughly liturgical process involving the emotional, intellectual, and bodily participation of each candidate for baptism and Eucharist. Through a process of formation and transformation understood to be contingent upon the agency of the Holy Spirit, the ancient catechesis aimed at nothing less than the enactment of the *participatio Christi*. Rather than elevating either cognition or affect, the process embraced both ways of knowing. By integrating regular instruction with participation in a wide range of liturgical actions, the church's faith became the new believer's faith. The church was understood as the site where the Holy Spirit enacts this transformation.

If the Protestant churches today are to take seriously the transmission of faith to our children and to new converts, we will need to overcome the modernist separation between cognition and emotion that still haunts our theologies and threatens the future of our churches. We have much to learn from the ancient catechesis, which placed Christian instruction in the context of the worshiping community of faith, where God the Holy Spirit is at work forming and transforming followers of Jesus Christ. Also, while some may be reluctant to admit it, the Pentecostal-Charismatic movement, which is the fastest growing branch of Christianity in the world, may have something very valuable to contribute to future ecumenical conversations. Clearly, there is a need for Christians to express and share our passion for Jesus Christ without being fanatical, and the reasonableness of our faith and doctrine without being legalistic.

41. Lehmann, *Ethics in a Christian Context*, 155.

4

Logos and Christian Witness: Ethical Discernment for Participation in God's Mission

The ***logos/witness*** *question:* If Israel's Writings offer a ***logos*** of accumulated communal wisdom about how to negotiate and renegotiate the tensions between sacred story, present experience, and eschatological promise, how and where is Christian love and care for neighbors in and beyond the faith community nurtured and renewed?

Answer: In the face of ever-changing personal, social, cultural, religious, and political realities, Christians discern together how best to love and care for their neighbors, thereby giving **witness** to Jesus Christ as participants in God's mission in the world. In Christian witness, the focus is on Jesus Christ, the Word of God, in his office as sage-king.

THE SLOW BUT STEADY rise of Christianity in the Greco-Roman world is estimated by sociologist Rodney Stark to have stood at 1.9 percent of the population in 250, at 10.5 percent by 300, and at 56.5 percent by 350.[1] Looking back through the long centuries of Western Christendom, that rise may seem inevitable, and the demise of paganism a consequent triumph. In fact, as Stark points out, the growth of the church was "long and perilous. There were many

1. Stark, *Rise of Christianity*, 7.

crisis points when different outcomes could easily have followed . . . But the fact remains that paganism did pass into history."[2]

Beginning with the question of how the early church triumphed over paganism, Stark examines a range of sociological factors that contributed to the success of the new religion, including conversion, the class basis of early Christianity, the mission to the Jews, expressions of benevolence during epidemics, the role of women in the church, the urban crisis, martyrdom, organization, and morality. While many social scientists are reluctant to take faith claims seriously, except perhaps as consequences of certain social factors, Stark bravely concludes that it was the doctrines of Christianity that shaped social realities, not the other way around.

> Surely doctrine was central to nursing the sick during times of plague, to the rejection of abortion and infanticide, to fertility, and to organizational vigor. Therefore, as I conclude this study, I find it necessary to confront what appears to me to be *the ultimate factor* in the rise of Christianity.
>
> Let me state my thesis: *Central doctrines of Christianity prompted and sustained attractive, liberating, and effective social relations and organizations.*[3]

It may seem obvious that what a religious community believes will have an impact on how that community lives. Nevertheless, given the modernist tendency to see religion more as a product rather than as a motivator of social change, the positive reciprocity Stark finds between Christian teaching and social ethics has been obscured in the educational ministries of Protestant churches that are divided into the often mutually exclusive subjectivist, activist, and objectivist orientations described in chapter 1.

Given the radical claims of the Gospel of Jesus Christ, it is not surprising that the early Christian communities defined themselves as possessing a distinctive mission *within*, *in contrast to*, and sometimes *in sharp tension with* their sociocultural milieu. The New Testament reflects all three dimensions of this relationship

2. Stark, *Rise of Christianity*, 93–94.

3. Stark, *Rise of Christianity*, 209–11.

to culture. For example, in Matthew's Gospel, Jesus speaks of his followers as "the salt of the earth" and "the light of the world" (Matt 5:13–14), underlining the preserving and illuminating function of a faith community *within* its social context. In what is thought to be his earliest letter, Paul admonishes the Thessalonians to maintain a distinctive, God-pleasing lifestyle *in contrast to* and *in tension with* "Gentiles who do not know God" and to "behave properly toward outsiders" (see 1 Thess 4:1–12). While the *agapē* ethic of redemptive love was first learned and practiced within the Christian community, its effects were naturally correlated to all of life's relations. Indeed, the motivation for the Gentile mission was the conviction that the promises of God to Israel were now extended in Jesus Christ and the Holy Spirit to all peoples. Themselves the consequence of cross-cultural missionary activity, the earliest churches understood themselves as missional communities, not as hermetic and esoteric religious enclaves. Within the complex religious milieu of the first century, there were times when lines between the church and the surrounding society had to be clearly drawn. For example, when writing to the Corinthians, Paul warns, "Do not be mismatched with unbelievers. For what partnership is there between righteousness and lawlessness? Or what fellowship is there between light and darkness?" (2 Cor 6:14).

From New Testament times, Christians have approached ethics in relation to the Gospel, not as some universal philosophical ethics. In contrast to ethical systems that begin with the establishment of some abstract universal principle or law and then proceed to apply these to individual cases, Christian ethics has a specific referent to the free and sovereign covenanting God who is revealed in Jesus Christ. H. R. Niebuhr speaks of Christian ethics as our *fitting response* to the action of God and, more specifically, as loving what God loves.[4] This *theo-ethical* logic goes like this: God

4. Niebuhr, *Responsible Self*, and *Purpose of the Church and Its Ministry*, 35–36. Joseph L. Allen' s thesis in *Love and Conflict* regarding Christian ethics is worth quoting: "(1) that God's being and action, as presented in the Christian proclamation, is to be understood as always and everywhere expressive of covenant love; (2) that the sense in which human beings are in the image of God finds its culmination in the capacity to enter into covenant with God

sends Christ to set a new direction for human life, and through the agency of the Holy Spirit, God leads Christians to live in the way of Jesus Christ. Seen as a gift of the divine-human relationality inaugurated and sustained by the grace of the free and sovereign God, the character of the Christian community is distinctive. Christ-like character is embodied, albeit provisionally, by the "afflicted but well-equipped" *witness* of the community of faith.[5]

Here we need to add some words of caution. First, from a biblical perspective, ethics has more to do with the witness of a community (i.e., the people of Israel, the kingdom of God, the ecclesia, the body of Christ) than with the witness of individual heroes or heroines of the faith. In Paul's letters to the churches, for example, communal discernment is a far more pressing pastoral and educational concern than the moral perfection of individuals. Second, we must be careful to avoid a common temptation to idealize the ethics of the first Christians. As ethicist Paul Lehmann points out, there was never a time when the church perfectly embodied its own ethical ideals.

> Unless we are prepared to say that the history of the church from the subapostolic times onwards is a history of defection from the original perfection of the primal Christian community, we have to face the fact that an analysis of Christian ethics involves a running conversation between the New Testament, on the one hand, and our situation, as heirs of the New Testament, on the other.[6]

Christian communities of every time and place engage in this "running conversation" by exegeting sacred text and exegeting local culture.

Third, the Gospel of salvation that pronounces and abolishes the sentence of death in a crucified and risen Savior rules out any possibility of moral perfection grounded in human agency. The

---

and one another; (3) that following the pattern of God's being and action, the pattern of human selfhood and action should be one of covenant love" (*Love and Conflict*, 54–55).

5. Barth, *Church Dogmatics*, 481.

6. Lehmann, *Ethics in a Christian Context*, 29.

God who justifies is the God who sanctifies his people after the pattern of Jesus Christ. Though always falling short of the mark, Christians understand themselves as empowered by the Spirit to bear witness to Jesus Christ among those within and beyond the fellowship of the church.[7]

Witness is the shape of Christian participation in the mission of God. The growth of the church within the cultural and religious diversity of the Roman Empire suggests that, even in spite of sporadic persecutions, Christians did not focus on themselves or their private religious experience. Beginning with the Gentile mission of Paul and his associates, they saw the body of Christ extending the mission of Jesus Christ into the world. Given this bold vision, it is no surprise that the young missionary community sometimes found itself in conflict with the values of the surrounding culture. In fact, Christian ethical reflection was born within the tensions of Gospel, church, and culture. How should Christians live in light of the Gospel? How should the churches nurture the community in its distinctive ethical identity? What obligations do Christians bear for their non-Christian neighbors? What should Christians do in times of social crisis?

In what follows, I will try to show how the catechumenate functioned as an institution for the communal discernment, transmission, and renewal of ethical identity in the early church. We will not proceed chronologically but will begin by exploring the *Didache*, an ethically oriented, early second-century document associated with the catechumenate.[8] Then we will go back to the New Testament and consider the role of *paraenesis* (ethical

7. Stark (*Rise of Christianity*, 212–13) sees this Christian commitment to love those beyond one's family and tribe as "the cultural basis for the revitalization of a Roman world groaning under a host of miseries . . . A major way in which Christianity served as a revitalization movement within the empire was in offering a coherent culture that was *entirely stripped of ethnicity.* All were welcome without need to dispense with ethnic ties."

8. A more sophisticated *paraenesis* is seen in the other literature associated with the catechumenate, namely, the *Apostolic Tradition* (early third century), Cyril's *Catechetical Lectures* (mid-fourth century), and Augustine's *First Catechetical Instruction* (early fifth century). For the sake of space, however, we will focus on the *Didache*, since it is the first specimen after Paul.

admonitions) in Paul's letters. We take this approach because the *Didache* presents a sharp, cautionary contrast to the *paraenesis* of the Pauline epistles.

In his doctoral dissertation, published as *The Doctrine of Grace in the Apostolic Fathers*, T. F. Torrance agrees with K. E. Kirk's characterization of the *Didache*.

> St. Paul's indignant wonder was evoked by the reversion of a small province [Galatia] of the Christian Church to the legalistic spirit of the Jewish religion. Had he lived half a century later, his cause for amazement would have been increased a hundredfold. The example of the Galatians might be thought to have infected the entire Christian Church; writer after writer seems to have little other interest than to express the genius of Christianity wholly in terms of law and obedience, reward and punishment. The mysterious document known as the *Didache* is as clear an example of this tendency as could be desired.[9]

The way that the *Didache* wanders from the grace of God proclaimed by Paul is highly instructive for the fragmented Protestant churches today. Our point is to show that, while ethical teaching played an important role in the formation of the earliest Christian communities, without the counterbalances of vibrant worship and wonder, ethical teaching easily devolves into forms of legalism or moralism that are alien to the grace of God in Jesus Christ and undermine Christian witness in the world.

The *Didache*, a document discovered in Jerusalem in 1873, is often cited as the first extrabiblical source related to the catechesis of the ancient church. Though debates on its authorship, place, and date continue, the general consensus places it at the beginning of the second century, perhaps around 120–130 CE. While it was likely used in the preparation of candidates for baptism, it does not necessarily reflect the universal practice of the churches in the early second century. It seems wisest to take it as one local source. According to O. C. Edwards,

9. Kirk, *Vision of God*, 111, quoted in Torrance, *Doctrine of Grace in the Apostolic Fathers*, 37.

> This document developed over quite a long period and thus it is never possible to say that all of its provisions were observed at any one time. Nevertheless, Robert Grant has been able to reconstruct this general picture of community practices: pre-baptismal ethical instruction and fasting, baptism in the three-fold name (administered in one of several ways) followed immediately by anointing and the Eucharist, fasting twice a week, Sunday corporate worship, the use of the Lord's Prayer, and other matters.[10]

We will look only at the prebaptismal ethical instruction ("the two ways of life and death"), since this material was most likely addressed directly to catechumens.[11] The opening section of the longer division on the "way of life" (fifty-eight verses) is a list of virtues and vices. The material is drawn mainly, but not exclusively, from the Old and New Testaments. It begins with the "first commandment" (Matt 22:37–38) and the Golden Rule (Matt 7:12). Drawing primarily on the Sermon on the Mount, catechumens are exhorted to love enemies and to give generously. The words themselves are not the problem as much as the interpretive framework. According to Torrance,

> The interesting thing is that while the *Didache* claims to go back to the words of our Lord, these are torn out of their context and fitted into another scheme in which they lose their original force and meaning. In the New Testament the Old was brought in to supply the needed categories with which to interpret the person and death of Christ, not in order to use its formal precepts as the grounding of the Christian life.[12]

When we look at the Pauline *paraenesis* below, we will return to Torrance's incisive point about the Christocentric reading of the Old Testament.

10. Edwards, "New Testament Church: From Jesus to the Apologists," 39–40. See also Robert Grant, "Development of the Christian Catechumenate," in Center for Liturgical Research, *Made, Not Born*, 32–49.

11. See *Teaching of the Twelve Apostles*.

12. Torrance, *Doctrine of Grace*, 38–39.

Continuing under the heading of the "way of life," the next section launches into a long list of negative commands taken mainly from the Decalogue (referred to as the "second commandment: forbidding gross sin") but including a liberal sprinkling of extrabiblical injunctions, for example, against pederasty and abortion.[13] As we will see later, while this blending of biblical and contemporary ethical subject matter is a common feature of Pauline *paraenesis*, the hermeneutic is very different.

Continuing under the general heading "way of life," the next section contains a long list of "evil things" to avoid because of their dire consequences (i.e., anger, jealousy, and quarrelsomeness lead to murder; lust to fornication; dirty talk and haughty eye to adultery; omens, enchantment, and astrology to idolatry; lying, money-loving, and vainglory to theft; murmuring, selfishness, and evil-mindedness to blasphemy). This section closes with a contrasting list of the positive virtues of the Christian: meekness, long-suffering, mercy, guilelessness, gentleness, humility, and accepting trials as from God.[14] Here again, Torrance rightly criticizes the document's lack of a doctrine of salvation and gratitude for God's grace.

> While it is not mentioned, it is possible that the death of Christ, like the rite of baptism, has only retrospective significance. At any rate it is not realised that pardon and justification are the present possession of the believer in Christ. Therefore the baptised believer is under obligation to strive to live in such a way as will keep him blameless and void of offence, knowing the reward of the righteous. By becoming a Christian a man only sets foot on the right way which he must follow through to the end in order to be saved. Salvation therefore is thrown forward to the future and tends to be regarded in terms of reward to righteous living. Because the believer is not already justified by the grace of God, he must justify himself.
>
> Another factor enters into this situation: that sin is not generally thought of in terms of guilt but rather

13. *Teaching of the Twelve Apostles*, 377.

14. *Teaching of the Twelve Apostles*, 378.

> in terms of corruption. This is why the emphasis is laid on immortality or incorruptibility. If sin is corruption, then doubtless salvation from sin will not come until after death. It follows then that if at baptism the believer does not put on salvation right away, Christ has not borne the whole burden of sin. There is still much left for the believer to do.[15]

Given that church leaders across the ages have far too often laid impossible ethical burdens and demands on the faithful, we should not be surprised by this early document's legalistic and moralistic tone. Whenever a community's experience of God's love, mercy, and grace is deficient, Christian ethical teaching can easily morph into a frightening, trauma-inducing moralistic perfectionism. Ironically, purportedly in the interest of sponsoring greater holiness, such teaching actually turns the community's attention to the self instead of to the One who saves and makes whole. When the Gospel proclamation and teaching of the all-sufficient grace of God in Jesus Christ is not front and center, the church opts for checklists like the ones in the *Didache*.[16]

The final section under the heading of "the way of life" encourages praying for and respecting church leaders (see Heb 13:7), recognizing the Lord's presence where the Lord's rule is proclaimed, attending worship, keeping peace in the community of faith, joyfully giving to those in need, teaching one's own children the fear of God, treating your slaves well (for slave-owners, see Eph 6:9 and Col 4:1), obeying your master (for slaves, see Eph 6:5 and Col 3:22), hating hypocrisy, keeping the commandments, and confessing one's sins in church.[17] While there is nothing in this final section that deviates from the content of the New Testament *paraenesis*, the lack of any sense of the interdependence of ethics, worship, and studied reflection on Scripture and church teaching is a striking contrast to what we read in Paul's letters.

15. Torrance, *Doctrine of Grace*, 40–41.

16. See, for example, Gal 3:1–5.

17. *Teaching of the Twelve Apostles*, 378.

The much shorter division of the "way of death" (fourteen verses) begins with a list of the following twenty-two sins: murder, adultery, lust, fornication, theft, idolatry, magic arts, witchcraft, rape, lying, hypocrisy, double-heartedness, deceit, haughtiness, depravity, self-will, greediness, filthy talking, jealousy, overconfidence, loftiness, and boastfulness. Catechumens are warned to "be delivered from all these." This list is by and large a repetition of the earlier section on "evil things." Here the list is followed by an explicit description of the social consequences of such vices: "[you will become] persecutors of good . . . pursuing requitals, not pitying a poor man, not laboring for the afflicted, . . . turning away from him who is in want, afflicting him that is distressed, advocates of the rich, lawless judges of the poor." Concern for mistreatment of the poor and the weak is grounded upon the theological conviction that such oppression is a denial of the creator God and God's human "handiwork." The "way of death" closes with an admonition to be faithful to the *Didache*, "since apart from God it teaches you," and a final warning about strictly avoiding food sacrificed to idols.[18]

Modern Protestants reared on the doctrines of grace and freedom of conscience will be put off by the moralistic and legalistic tone of the *Didache*. But before dismissing it out of hand, we should also wonder why the community in front of this document felt they had to be so precise about certain behaviors. The simple answer is that these behaviors were likely common both in the surrounding society and in the community of faith, therefore church leaders felt hard-pressed to draw clear distinctions. It is easy for us to forget that, until the beginning of the fourth century, the tiny minority churches were in a precarious missional situation,[19] often finding their religious identity in tension with the local culture. From the standpoint of the *Didache*'s early second-century community, the eventual "triumph" of Christianity over Roman

18. *Teaching of the Twelve Apostles*, 379.

19. Stark (*The Rise of Christianity*, 7) estimates that in the year 100 CE, Christians constituted 0.0126 percent of the Greco-Roman world; by 150, the figure had risen to 0.07 percent.

paganism was totally unimaginable. In this situation, the church could not ignore questions about family life, work, speech, economics, and political power, which are also treated in Scripture. From our distance, it is easy to disparage the community that wrote the *Didache* for its impoverished theology; that is, where is their sense of grace and the assurance of salvation? But we should also remember that the pre-Nicaean churches did not have the benefit of a clear doctrinal consensus. In such a fraught missional situation, the temptation for improvisation was very strong. From our distance, especially in light of the collapse of European Christendom and Protestant hegemony in the United States, perhaps we might attend more closely to the missional struggle, if not the conclusions, of the *Didache*. In this document, we hear the voice of a beleaguered minority community striving to discern the ethical implications of the Gospel in the midst of cultural and religious pluralism.

* * *

Before turning to *paraenesis* in Paul, I want to say a word about an unresolved issue in Protestant churches today. Since the twentieth century, there has been a tendency in some quarters of the church to see the ministry of the Word exclusively in terms of the proclamation/preaching of the *kerygma*. This tendency has led to a devaluation of the slower, time-intensive educational work of the churches in practices of catechesis, spiritual formation, or discipleship.[20] This rupture between proclamation and nurture has led to an elevation of preaching over teaching as the core ministry of the Word. Coupled with the legacy of the lay-led Sunday School movement, which focused largely on the biblical education of children, the church's teaching ministry, as a legitimate and vital aspect of the ministry of the Word, has been de-emphasized or neglected. When the *kerygma-didachē* binary

20. Roman Catholics and some Protestants use "catechesis"; "spiritual formation" is replacing "Christian education"; and "discipleship" is favored by evangelicals.

is taken to an extreme, God's gracious action in Jesus Christ is associated only with the proclamation of the cross and resurrection, and as a result, the *didachē* of Jesus and the Pauline *paraenesis* are demoted to second-class status.

The triumph of the preaching ministry over the teaching ministry in the Protestant churches is seen clearly in the relative social status afforded to pastors and church educators. Today, in contexts such as Japan, where the influence of modern Western theology is so strong, teaching ministry is seen as a laudable human effort but is related only tangentially, if at all, to the inbreaking of the Spirit believed to accompany the proclamation of the Word, that is, in the Sunday sermon. I believe that this divorce of teaching and preaching is a serious departure from the New Testament and the churches rooted in the Reformation.

The letters of Paul are not stand-alone lectures, sermons, treatises, or exhortations. On the contrary, they freely weave together Gospel-centered *kerygma* (proclamation), *paraenesis* (ethical exhortation), and *didachē* (teaching/doctrine) in ways one would expect from a first-century Jew immersed in the holistic epistemology of Torah, Prophets, and Writings. Furthermore, while the churches Paul established included Jews of the diaspora who had confessed Jesus as the Messiah, his letters arise from his apostolic, missionary ministry among Gentile converts, who had little or no knowledge of Israel's Scriptures. Arising from the matrix of Israel's sacred texts, the Pauline letters seamlessly integrate elements of proclamation, exhortation, and doctrine, while focusing laser-like on the radically new event of Jesus Christ. Furthermore, they are occasioned by the specific missional and pastoral concerns of the churches.

As one example, when we explore Paul's view of the relationship between salvation in Christ (justification) and growth in Christ (sanctification), we glean from his epistles echoes of the canonical integration of Torah, Prophets, and Writings. Unlike certain readers who, following Luther, see justification of faith as the lodestar of Pauline teaching, I see instead an ordered simultaneity between justification and sanctification. To wit, while Paul was an innovator, he gives priority to the received tradition and confession about Jesus (*paradosis*) in his presentation of the core Gospel confession (esp. 1 Cor 15:1–8). Paul's ethical exhortations are predicated on the received tradition and confession about Jesus Christ. In theological terms, we may say that justification "in Christ" is the basis for sanctification "in Christ." In plain terms, what God does in Jesus Christ sets the direction of how we should live as followers of Jesus. The order of Paul's logic is irreversible: *paraenesis* flows from *paradosis*. According to Bornkamm, "The interrelatedness of word of salvation and calling on the one hand and obedience, summons, and demand on the other has a particular significance for Paul."[21] To put it yet another way, the Gospel of Jesus Christ is the singular presupposition for instruction in the Christian life. Or in the simplest terms, we love and care for others because Jesus first loved and cared for us.

In sharp contrast to the *Didache*, Pauline ethics knows no ground independent of the divine grace of justification and sanctification in Jesus Christ. Paul makes no attempt to approach ethics philosophically, applying some fixed universal laws to particular situations. And he does not place impossible ethical demands on the community. For Paul, all time—past, present, and future—has been transformed by the crucified, risen, and coming Lord. The gracious Lord who justifies is the same gracious Lord who sanctifies, enabling forgiven sinners to love and care for others, thereby participating in God's mission in the world.

To draw another contrast to the *Didache*: Paul invariably casts his ethical teaching in an eschatological light. That is, instead of burdening the individual with an impossible list of moral injunctions about how to live, as in the *Didache*, Paul portrays the life and character of a community—which is being made holy and just (sanctified) by and for a holy and just God—in joyful anticipation of Christ's gracious judgment at the end of time. This hope-filled eschatological orientation, which infuses Paul's letters and indeed the entire New Testament, has become an embarrassment to many modern Protestants, who are rightly wary about

21. Bornkamm, *Paul*, 202.

pop-culture eschatologies that manipulate and frighten the gullible. But I see the loss of the joyful and hope-filled eschatological dimension of the Gospel as one cause for the lack of emphasis on communal ethical discernment in so many Protestant churches today. When Christian ethics is unmoored from the blessed hope and relegated solely to private matters of conscience, the robust public witness of the Christian community suffers.

Let us now look at two characteristic Pauline texts that show how ethical admonitions flow from the Gospel. As Paul's argument against antinomianism in Romans 6 shows, God's grace in Jesus Christ, while negating every form of legalism, enables those who have been baptized into Christ's death and resurrection to walk "in newness of life."

> What then are we to say? Should we continue in sin in order that grace may abound? By no means! How can we who died to sin go on living in it? Do you not know that all of us who have been baptized into Christ Jesus were baptized into his death? Therefore we have been buried with him by baptism into death, so that, just as Christ was raised from the dead by the glory of the Father, so we too might walk in newness of life. (Rom 6:1–4)

Commenting on this "new life," Bornkamm says,

> It is not sufficient to think of the new life to which the admonitions summon the Christian as a mere supplementary effect of faith; in itself it is a mode of faith, an appropriation of what God has already assigned. The believer's actions derive from God's act, and the decisions taken by obedience from God's antecedent decision for the world in Christ. Thus, the two come together in equilibrium: to live on the basis of *grace*, but also to *live* of the basis of grace.[22]

The gift of divine grace bears fruit in communal and personal life. As the larger context makes clear, "newness of life" or "sanctification" does not mean moral perfection. Instead, it refers primarily to being set aside by God for God's purposes. Thus, just as in

22. Bornkamm, *Paul*, 202–03.

justification, God alone is the Subject of Christian sanctification. As a grateful recipient of God's sanctifying love, the community of faith proleptically bears the fruit of eternal life (Rom 6:22). But the relative maturity of the fruit itself is never a proper focus of attention. Christians depart from Paul whenever we make distinctions between the more or less sanctified. Nor is sanctification in Paul a hierarchy of progressive spiritual stages or steps. As needy recipients of and participants in God's extravagant grace, those who are in Christ always stand on the same level ground.

In terms that may make pious Christians blush with embarrassment, Paul is brutally honest in his description of the fierce personal battle he experienced: "Wretched man that I am! Who will rescue me from this body of death?" (Rom 7:24). To draw ethical distinctions among Christians is to take a fatal detour from God's grace; it is to draw attention away from the divine Subject of sanctification, who alone can save, to its human recipient, who can only respond with joyful thanks and praise to what God has done. Again, in contrast to the *Didache*, Paul's emphasis is on the gracious triumph of divine agency over human agency. Indeed, in Romans 8 Paul portrays the fullness of Christian redemption in the context of the "groaning" of "the whole creation!" (vv. 22–23).[23]

Sanctification is always provisional because its fulfillment is circumscribed by the mystery of Christ's coming in the *eschaton*. Though righteousness is always God's free gift, this does not mean that the community is free from making a determined effort to discern the will of God in present circumstances. Paul freely admits that his own knowledge of Christ's resurrection and death was incomplete. "I press on toward the goal for the prize of the heavenly call of God in Christ Jesus. Let those of us then who are mature be of the same mind; and if you think differently about anything, this too God will reveal to you" (Phil 3:14–15). Though

23. As the Scot's Confession puts it, "To put this even more plainly; as we willingly disclaim any honor and glory for our own creation and redemption, so do we willingly also for our regeneration and sanctification; for by ourselves we are not capable of thinking one good thought, but he who has begun the work in us alone continues us in it, to the praise and glory of his undeserved grace" (Office of the General Assembly, "Scot's Confession," 12.3.12).

the metaphor is taken from athletics, Paul is not suggesting that Christian maturity has anything to do with Christian competition or comparisons of relative holiness. Rather, Christian maturity is determined in relation to the single referent of "the heavenly call of God in Christ Jesus" (v. 14). Paul's confidence in God's revelation (v. 15b) does not mean, however, that the Christian's relation to Christ is ever a purely individual matter.

On the contrary, instead of relegating the Christian's relation to Christ to individual religious experience and conscience, Paul makes the surprising claim that this relationality is reflected in the concrete experience of the community of faith. "Brothers and sisters, join in imitating me, and observe those who live according to the example you have in us" (Phil 3:17; cf. 1 Cor 4:16; 11:1; 1 Thess 1:6).[24] Put simply, Christians learn to follow Christ by following other Christians who, however imperfectly, follow Christ.[25] Notice that here again, as in Romans, the ethical life of the Christian community is described within the context of the eschatological expectation. Again, we see here that Christian ethical life has a provisional character precisely because it is neither the self-grounded source of its present strength nor its future fulfillment. Rather, Christian life is empowered by the crucified, risen, and coming Lord, who "will transform the body of our humiliation that it may be conformed to the body of his glory" (v. 21).

In the same context, Paul tearfully admonishes his readers about certain people, evidently with considerable influence within the church, who "live as enemies of the cross of Christ. I have often told you of them, and now I tell you even with tears. Their end is their destruction; their god is the belly; and their glory is in their shame; their minds are set on earthly things" (Phil 3:18–19). Thus,

24. See also 1 Cor 4:16 and 11:1, also 1 Thess 1:6.

25. As a sociologist, Stark (*The Rise of Christianity*, 16–17) says that this horizontal dimension of interpersonal relationships was also an important contributing factor in conversion. He concludes that people converted to the new faith when their "*interpersonal attachments to members of that religious group overbalanced their attachments to nonmembers.* In effect, conversion is not about seeking or embracing an ideology; it is about bringing one's religious behavior into alignment with that of one's friends and family members."

a present polemical situation becomes an opportunity for the community to recall the true source of its life and ultimate judgment and, in a process of communal discernment, to reflect upon and clarify its ethical commitments.[26]

Paul's view of the Gospel of Jesus Christ encompasses both the tradition of *remembrance* of God's action in the cross and resurrection and the tradition of *anticipation* of the parousia. The events of salvation history and hope provide the direction of Christian life. Nevertheless, in regard to the specific "content" of Paul's ethical teaching, he draws freely in an *ad hoc* manner on traditional Jewish and contemporary Greek cultural resources. According to Bornkamm,

> In enumerating the practical implication of such Christian life in "obedience," "service," and "indebtedness," Paul in his admonitions quite deliberately employs current concepts and expressions which everyone understood, and makes no effort at all to work out a new, specifically Christian, scale of values. This is particularly apparent in the numerous loose and not systematically ordered lists in his admonitions, which in form and content have direct parallels in the catalogues of "virtues and vices" in the Jewish tradition as found in Proverbs and in Hellenistic popular ethical teaching (cf. Rom 1:29–31; 12:8–21; 13:13; 1 Cor 5:10f.; 6:9f.; 2 Cor 12:20f.; Gal 5:19-23).[27]

Paul's apparent freedom in utilizing familiar contemporary and traditional ethical themes should encourage Christian communities in different cultural circumstances to take a hard look at how

26. What Paul is doing here and what the church has always done as it has defined itself in contrast with other cultural realities can be understood sociologically in Berger and Luckmann's term "symbolic universe." "The symbolic universe . . . locates all collective events in a cohesive unity that includes past, present and future. With regard to the past, it establishes a 'memory' that is shared by all the individuals socialized within the collectivity. With regard to the future, it establishes a common frame of reference for the projection of individual actions" (Berger and Luckmann, *Social Construction of Reality*, 103).

27. Bornkamm, *Paul*, 203.

well we relate the Gospel to the specific ethical issues confronting our societies and cultural settings.

Furthermore, the methods of argumentation that Paul uses in his *paraenesis* reveal a freedom and creativity in his ethical imperatives. Bornkamm continues, "Going through the parenetic sections from letter to letter, it is amazing to see the variety of and differences in the apostle's *argumentation* in each case—absolutely no set form or cliches; in other words, he appeals to his hearers' and readers' understanding and does not simply proclaim and decree."[28] Paul's interpretive freedom invites today's pastors and church educators to engage their own cultural context with missional artistry.

If Paul displays a degree of freedom when employing relevant ethical subjects and methods of argumentation, this does not mean that there was nothing new in his ethical teaching. Once again, Bornkamm says,

> The new thing here is not the subject matter, but rather the content of the admonitions: the whence and wither of the road on which Christians are under way; the grace from which they derive their lives and in virtue of which they are summoned to a new service and obedience, and the coming day of Christ, for which they are "called" to "obtain salvation" (1 Thess 4:7; 5:9). They, too, have to give account of themselves before God, the just judge, on that "day" (Rom 14:12; 1 Cor 4:5; 2 Cor 5:10, etc.).[29]

This description of the journey *from grace, in grace,* and *to grace* describes very clearly what is new and what is at stake in Christian ethical teaching.

It may be tempting to conclude from the above that communal deliberation on ethical matters is a vital matter only in churches that take the eschatological expectation seriously. On this point, a note of clarification and caution needs to be sounded. Unfortunately, as we already mentioned, the church's confession, "He will come again in glory to judge the living and the dead,"

28. Bornkamm, *Paul*, 204.

29. Bornkamm, *Paul*, 204.

has been twisted by many into a hell-threatening apocalypticism. Fear-inducing preaching and teaching, which utilizes spurious timelines to outline the historical events that will precede or accompany the Lord's coming, has more of the spirit of Enlightenment rationalism than Pauline *paraenesis*. For others, the parousia may be reduced to some future ideological or political triumph over injustice. Some still believe that human effort will bring about the kingdom of God on earth. Another child of an Enlightenment view of progress, this view also misses the Christocentric view of Paul, which, from start to finish, is grounded in the agency of the crucified, risen, and coming Lord Jesus Christ.

In Paul, we find no speculation about dates and no correlation with any ideological or political movement—in short, no attempt to press the mystery of the parousia into the service of some rational scheme or higher consciousness. For Paul, the day of Christ has an actuality that stands over and against all other actualities, an actuality every bit as real as the cross and the resurrection. That day casts a gracious proleptic light, not a dark fearful shadow, over the history of the Christian community and its individual members. Out of this conviction comes a need to exercise great care in reminding the churches that we live in the light of a radical hope. The mystery of the parousia is a call to joyful expectation and to communal ethical discernment about how best to live in light of that day. As an essential dimension of the ministry of the Word, the ethical discernment helps Christians participate in the mission of God now and to joyfully anticipate the day when we will see "face to face" (1 Cor 13:12).

5

Ethos and Christian Wonder: Identity Formation and Renewal for Participation in God's Mission

The ***ethos/wonder*** *question:* If the core ***ethos*** in Israel is mediated by its identity given in Torah, how and where does the Christian community learn its identity in relation to God and neighbor?

Answer: In intentional educational settings marked by practices of **wondering**, Christian communities grow in their understanding of the Gospel of Jesus Christ by studying and interrogating Scripture and church teaching. Here, the focus is on Jesus Christ, the Word of God, in his office as priest.[1]

THOUGH IT ALMOST GOES without saying, before any religious community can begin to nurture its children or new converts, that community must believe they are participants in a tradition worthy of being passed on, taught, renewed, and lived out with passion and courage. Thus, reaching some consensus about the contours of the received tradition and then handing it on are

1. The use of the word "ethical" or "ethic" here should not be confused with our prior use of the word *ethos*. When we refer to the *ethos* of the Torah or the Gospel, we mean "the characteristic spirit of the Jewish or Christian culture or community as manifested in its specific story, beliefs, and aspirations." When we say ethical, we mean "of or relating to the moral principles of a particular faith."

issues every new generation must face. For the earliest churches, the development of confessions of faith or creeds was a complicated process, marked by the struggle to find words appropriate to the God revealed in Israel and Jesus Christ. The process of mapping the boundaries of faith was refined by polemical issues that the followers of the Way encountered within the matrix of first-century Palestinian Judaism and the tensions they faced in the early missionary encounters within a variety of local cultures in and beyond the Roman Empire.

Largely as a result of the efforts of Paul and other early apostles, missionaries, evangelists, and teachers, Christianity moved beyond its roots in Judaism at a rather early stage. This expansion suggests the existence of a strong confessional identity or tradition of faith from a relatively early period. J. N. D. Kelly says, "Had the Christians of the apostolic age not conceived of themselves as possessing a body of distinctive, consciously held beliefs, they would scarcely have separated themselves from Judaism and undertaken an immense programme of missionary expansion."[2] Even the Apostle Paul, a charismatic interpreter of the received tradition, "had a healthy regard for the objective body of teaching authoritatively handed down in the Church."[3] While it is generally agreed that "Jesus is Lord" or "Christ is Lord" are likely the primitive forms of Christian confession, we observe a degree of confessional diversity, even if not development, within the New Testament itself.[4]

2. Kelly, *Early Christian Creeds*, 7.

3. Kelly, *Early Christian Creeds*, 10. As we saw in chapter 2, Paul stresses in 1 Cor 15:3 that he was passing on a tradition that he had received. Also see 1 Thess 1:6; 2 Thess 3:1; 1 Cor 14:36; Gal 6:6.

4. Refuting Cullman's attempt to discern, against the background of the church's expanding Gentile mission, an evolution in the New Testament from the one-membered "Jesus is Lord" or "Christ is Lord" into the binitarian terms of "Father of our Lord Jesus Christ," Kelly (*Early Christian Creeds*, 24) concludes that "one membered, two-membered and three-membered confessions flourished side by side in the apostolic Church as parallel and mutually independent formulations of the one kerygma; and this is a datum of prime importance [for later creedal developments]."

These apostolic expressions of the tradition would have been taught with reverence and treasured by new converts as a sacred gift, since, to the early Christians, apostolic authority was equated with Christ's authority.[5] We also know that the first churches were engaged in some form of catechesis, systematically handing on the tradition to converts and the next generation.[6] It appears that the appeal to a clear and authoritative tradition of faith was particularly strong in the period leading up to the fourth-century conciliar decisions on the doctrine of the Trinity and the establishment of the New Testament canon.

Such an appeal to authority can be seen, for example, in the early second-century *Didache*, or *Teaching of the Twelve Apostles*, possibly an early manual for catechumens, which we have already examined in chapter 4. Besides instruction on church practice, the *Didache* offers stringent moral injunctions by appealing to the sayings of Jesus and the Decalogue. However, as we saw in conversation with Torrance, this document lacks a doctrine of grace, and its negative character presents a sharp contrast to the positive pastoral advice found in Paul's letters. Later in the second century, Irenaeus refers to a *regula fides* (a summary of Christian doctrine likely used for catechetical purposes) that had apostolic authority. Irenaeus claims that, even if there had been no other writings from the apostles, the creedal tradition itself would have sufficed for teaching converts and refuting heretics.[7]

Like the *Shema Yisrael*, Christian confessions of faith were viewed as normative and binding on all members of the community of faith. In the earliest days, the practice of teaching a creed likely followed synagogue models, in which the creed was recited and expounded along with Scripture as part of a liturgy. The tradition summarized in creeds became a baseline of Christian identity, and like Israel's Torah, the Gospel was received as divine gift and as

5. Kelly, *Early Christian Creeds*, 22–23.

6. Kelly, *Early Christian Creeds*, 8. See Jude 3; 2 Tim 1:13; 4:3; Titus 1:9; Heb 6:2.

7. Irenaeus, *Against Heresies*, 3.4.1.

a nonnegotiable, reassuring fact of life transcending each generation while tying all generations together.

* * *

As we move into the first decades of the third century, we discover in the *Apostolic Tradition* an interrogatory confession of faith, perhaps with its roots in the creed of the Roman church, that had developed into a form with a remarkable resemblance to the later Apostle's Creed. Following a three-year period of instruction, each catechumen would be questioned by the bishop about his or her confession of God the Father, Son, and Holy Spirit.

> When each of them to be baptized has gone down into the water, the one baptizing shall lay hands on each of them, asking, "Do you believe in God the Father Almighty?" And the one being baptized shall answer, "I believe." He shall then baptize each of them once, laying his hand upon each of their heads. Then he shall ask, "Do you believe in Jesus Christ, the Son of God, who was born of the Holy Spirit and the Virgin Mary, who was crucified under Pontius Pilate, and died, and rose on the third day living from the dead, and ascended into heaven, and sat down at the right hand of the Father, the one coming to judge the living and the dead?" When each has answered, "I believe," he shall baptize a second time. Then he shall ask, "Do you believe in the Holy Spirit and the Holy Church and the resurrection of the flesh?" Then each being baptized shall answer, "I believe." And thus let him baptize the third time.[8]

What is fascinating here is the suggestion that, contrary to the view that the ancient creeds and confessions evolved out of the church's liturgy, the practice of catechetical instruction itself seems to have played a significant role in shaping these doctrinal summaries.[9] Kelly says, "It should be obvious that a wider background must be sought for *the brief confessions of faith* than the

8. Hippolytus, *Apostolic Tradition* 21:12–18.

9. Kelly, *Early Christian Creeds*, 13.

actual ceremony of baptism itself. Their roots lie not so much in the Christian's sacramental initiation into the Church as in the catechetical training by which it was preceded."[10] Again, according to Turner, "The Creed belongs, not indeed to the administration of the rite of Baptism, but to the preparation for it."[11] If this view is correct, then it seems reasonable to see the early church's catechetical practice as an example of constructive practical theological reasoning, with Christian practice guiding theory/theology rather than the other way around.

Skipping ahead another one hundred years, by the time of Cyril's *Catechetical Lectures* (around 350), the baptismal creed had achieved full stature as the "core text" in the prebaptismal instruction of catechumens. The *traditio symboli* ("handing over of the creed") was a solemn rite conducted during the fifth lecture, when the bishop passed on the sacred creed to each candidate. Evoking a sense of awe and wonder, the presiding bishop proclaims,

> In learning the Faith and in professing it, acquire and keep that [the creed] only, which is now delivered to thee by the Church, and which has been built up strongly out of all the Scriptures . . . This summary I wish you both to commit to memory when I recite it, and to rehearse it with all diligence among yourselves, not writing it out on paper, but engraving it by the memory upon your heart.[12]

Each candidate was thus expected to memorize the creed and, during the last lecture, would recite it back to the bishop during a second rite called the *redditio symboli* ("rehearsal or delivery of the creed").[13] When we consider that most adult catechumens could not read Scripture on their own, it is not surprising that so much weight was attributed to these doctrinal summaries during the initiation into the church.

10. Kelly, *Early Christian Creeds*, 50.

11. Turner, *History and Use of Creed*, 17.

12. Cyril, *Catechetical Lectures*, 5:12.

13. As in the time of Hippolytus, the creed was still not recited normally during the liturgy except in connection with baptism.

From the practices of the early church we have briefly examined thus far, we may make the following observations about the relation between the received tradition of faith and catechesis:

1. The Gospel represented by a creed was understood as a part of "received tradition," not as something each new generation had to deconstruct and reconstruct on their own.[14]
2. Baptismal creeds were treated as faithful summaries of the Gospel, as revealed in Scripture, and sufficient for nurturing new converts and the next generation.
3. Doctrinal summaries in a creed were carefully transmitted and taught to the faithful as aids in hearing and understanding the reading, proclamation, and explication of Scripture in worship.
4. The ritual acts of receiving and delivering the sacred creed must have created a sense of wonder, mystery, and awe that inspired the perceptions and reflections of the mostly adult catechumens.

We have suggested that, for Christians, the Gospel of Jesus Christ, as summarized in a creed, is analogous to the Torah in Israel. Commenting on Torah teaching in Israel, Brueggemann says, "There is no attempt to modernize, to make contemporary, to interpret, to link to any present issue . . . These convictions could be asserted in their boldness and left to stand. They would do their own work."[15]

In my view, Protestant churches today need to recover the nerve to confidently teach the Gospel as a sacred gift and with a joyful sense of wonder. Brueggemann goes on,

> Life must be a gift before it can be a task. It must be there waiting for us and not constructed by us, though eventually we may participate in the ongoing world construction . . . I dare say that much of the immobility of the

14. While such an idea may be abhorrent to certain churches with strong ties to nineteenth-century individualism and volunteerism, this view was shared by the churches of the Reformation.

15. Brueggemann, *Creative Word*, 20.

> church is because of a theological normlessness, Torahlessness, when everyone does whatever he or she pleases, except that soon our desire is skewed, emptied, failed and boring. The Torah is the line drawn against the darkness and disorder, against the Canaanites and Egyptians, but finally against the chaos and death that awaits.[16]

To repeat, the Gospel of Jesus Christ is the Christian analogue to Israel's Torah. The Gospel, not some other story, is what binds the World Christian movement together in "one holy, catholic, and apostolic church." The Gospel is never our possession, but it is to be received and passed on with thoughtfulness, joy, creativity, and wonder. As the "cognitive matrix" through which Scripture is heard and interpreted by the community of faith, it challenges the mind, reverberates in the heart, and inspires joyful discipleship.

Whereas *worship* centers on the God of redeeming love, and *witness* is the outpouring of God's redeeming love for the world through well-equipped but flawed human beings, *wonder*, which combines a sense of awe with critical thinking and imagination, is the intellectual and aesthetic disposition of Christian worshippers and witnesses as they read and meditate on Scripture and church teaching, interpreting the Gospel of Jesus Christ in their particular languages, cultures, places, and times. In humble recognition of the incompleteness of our current understanding and in hopeful anticipation of the fullness of time and the gathering up of all things—in heaven and earth—in Christ (Eph 1:10), the intellectual and aesthetic disposition of wonder helps to sustain the vitality of the church's worship and witness.

16. Brueggemann, *Creative Word*, 21.

Concluding Comments on the World Christian Movement

HAVING LIVED AND WORKED in Japan as a mission coworker and pastoral educator for over twenty years, I have experienced on a personal level how a shared story and mutual understanding are necessary for a community's survival. Stumbling through the long and arduous process of learning Japanese, a radically different language from my native American English, I often experienced the frustrating and isolating void of communication breakdown. In spite of our best efforts, most missionaries, like exiles, refugees, and immigrants, never manage to achieve the linguistic competence of native speakers. There are countless times when we inadvertently say the wrong thing or incorrectly interpret what is said to us. Other times we cannot quite grasp a speaker's total message or adequately convey the nuances of our own thoughts in our second language. This communication gap inevitably creates a relational distance.

Indeed, no community can survive for long without a shared language and story. But as anyone who has shared a committed long-term relationship will attest, even the closest partners who share the same language and story communicate only in proximate, indirect terms. Shared language and story are not enough, because sometimes one's intended message is miscommunicated (*mis-given*). Without thinking, I may blurt out to my wife, child, brother, or friend, "What a ridiculous thing to say!" when what I should have said, "I don't understand" or "I feel hurt by what you said." At other times, one's message is misinterpreted (*mis-taken*). In what I may take as a moment of honest self-disclosure, I say, "I feel hurt by what you said." But this time the listener hears judgment: "You've lost control!"

With the risk of *mis-giving* and *mis-taking* always before us, faith in the deeper, hidden reality of cruciform love that binds us together beyond our convoluted intentions is indispensable for Christian communities. Our relationality "in Christ" is a gift to be received, not a goal to be accomplished. While language, which sometimes reveals and sometimes conceals, helps us negotiate the stormy waters of our muddled intentions and perceptions, over time we learn that "love covers a multitude of sins" (1 Pet 4:8).

How might trust in an underlying love beyond our mutually shared meanings work for Protestant churches that are divided into subjectivist, activist, and objectivist silos? Whether we belong to more liberal, more radical, or more orthodox churches, or whether we are from Africa, Asia, Europe, Latin America, the Middle East, North America, or Oceania, we who belong to Christ bear his name in our common baptism. Through our death, burial, and resurrection with Christ, expressed in baptism and confession of faith (Col 2:11–14), we enjoy a radically new relationship with God in Christ. Being called Christian signifies this *new humanity*, established by God in Christ and in the power of the Holy Spirit. Christian identity is a gracious gift of God. Our new name is also a sign that we have been intimately joined to a community that Ephesians describes as "the household of God, built on the foundation of the apostles and prophets, with Christ Jesus himself as the cornerstone" (Eph 2:19b–20). The churches, which exist in countless local instantiations with different liturgical, ethical, and theological emphases in different times and cultures, is one in Christ by the grace of God. In this global digital age, the World Christian movement must not take lightly the divine gift of our unity in Christ.

At the same time, as members of this worldwide community in Christ, we continue to embody and express our particular cultural identities. According to Stark, one of the most important factors in the early spread of Christianity was the freedom for converts to the new religion to maintain their own ethnic identities. "In my judgment, a major way in which Christianity served as a revitalization movement within the [Roman] empire was in offering a coherent culture that was *entirely stripped of ethnicity*. All were welcome without the need to dispense with ethnic ties."[1]

The salient point here for the global church is that the Gospel of Christ, in spite of the many failings of church leaders, theologians, and missionaries, has evidenced an astounding ability to include peoples from so many of the world's different cultures. It is almost as if the heavenly vision of John is coming to pass in our own time![2] From the point of view of an eschatological faith, the redeemed humanity that the suffering, crucified, risen, ascended, and coming Son of God presents to the Father is a transformed humanity that embraces all of the historical and cultural differences found among human beings. This faith and this hope are expressed in the biblical symbols of the peaceable kingdom, the kingdom of God, or the family of God. Especially considering the improvement in technologies of transportation and communication, I sometimes wonder why Christians are not more eager to learn about and share the rich varieties of expressions of faith resident in the global church today.

Over long centuries, the staggering cultural diversity of the church has admittedly been the source of much misunderstanding, tension, and division. Too often, our spiritual unity in Christ

1. Stark, *Rise of Christianity*, 213.

2. "After this I looked, and there was a great multitude that no one could count, from every nation, from all tribes and peoples and languages, standing before the throne and before the Lamb, robed in white, with palm branches in their hands" (Rev 7:9). According to Stark's estimate (*Rise of Christianity*, 6–7), there were probably only a total of about 7,530 Christians, or 0.0126 percent of the population of the Roman Empire, around the time Revelation was written (100 CE). By 300, before the conversion of Constantine in 312, Stark gives an astounding figure of 6,299,832 Christians, or 10.5 percent of the population of the Roman Empire. (He arrives at this specific number by assuming a growth rate of 40 percent per decade, beginning with an estimate of 1,000 Christians in the year 40.)

has been pitted against our cultural diversity. This antagonism is of course related to the above-mentioned problem of language. For example, as a North American Protestant engaged in intercultural mission for more than twenty years in Japan, I must confess that it was much easier to believe that our unity in Christ is a better gift of God than is our cultural diversity. Even after mastering the language, there is a constant level of frustration in having to express myself in a very different way. To repeat, shared language is not enough to overcome our differences. But I wonder if now might not be a good time to reconceive our cultural and theological diversity as a good gift of God that, like our unity in Christ, has not yet been given adequate theological expression, especially in the West.

While Karl Barth did not live to see the twentieth century's complete demographic reversal of World Christianity from the Global North to the Global South, the implication of his words about faith are as staggering today as when he wrote them.

> Christian faith can and should be varied . . . Although its object, the Jesus Christ attested in Scripture and proclaimed by the community, is single, consistent and free from contradiction, yet for all His singularity and unity His form is inexhaustibly rich, so that it is not merely legitimate but obligatory that believers should continually see and understand it in new lights and aspects. For He Himself does not present Himself to them in one form but in many—indeed, He is not in Himself uniform but multiform. How can it be otherwise when He is the true Son of God who is eternally rich?[3]

Extending Barth's paradoxical point about the unity and multiformity of Jesus Christ into the current situation of world Christianity, I suggest that the Western churches that originally sent out missionaries around the world now have a sacred obligation to learn how Christians in the two-thirds or majority world are worshiping, witnessing, and wondering. This task will require that we take seriously the distinctive ways that people, with their differing

3. Barth, *Church Dogmatics*, 763.

conceptions of being human, experience their participation in Christ and his mission in the world. We may also be surprised to discover that the experiences of culturally different churches shed light on the earliest communities in front of the New Testament writings, as many analogous issues are repeated as the Gospel takes root in new cultural ground.[4]

Commenting on the unimaginable expansion of the church over the last two centuries, Scottish historian of Christian mission Andrew Walls has noted,

> We now live at a time when the church is multicultural. I think that the fullness of the stature of Christ will emerge only when Christians from all these cultures come together. If I understand what Paul says in Ephesians correctly, it is as though Christ himself is growing as the different cultures are brought together in him.[5]

The christological conviction underlying this obligation to "come together" is that a first-century Palestinian Jew, who is also the second person of the Holy Trinity, has assumed and embraced our humanity, not in some abstract sense, but in its actuality wherever it is lived, under the limiting personal, social, cultural, and political conditions of space and time. I wonder whether a renewed ecumenical consciousness may help us overcome our epistemological schisms?

If Protestant churches could somehow gain a renewed vision of divine praxis infusing the ecclesial practices of formation for participation in Christ and the mission of God, they perhaps could begin to move beyond our present divisions to nurture the common eschatological anticipation of the "fullness of the stature of Christ." In this book, I have described heuristic connections between ways of knowing in Old Testament Torah, Prophets, and Writings and New Testament *didachē*, *kerygma*, and *paraenesis*,

4. After I was officially appointed as a PC (USA) mission coworker to Japan, a wise Japanese pastor sat me down and said to me, "Welcome to Rome in AD 150." It took me years to grasp the profound meaning of his words.

5. Walls, "Expansion of Christianity," 795. The biblical reference is to Eph 4:1–16.

and we have explored further echoes of this tripartite canonical epistemology in the catechumenate of the early churches. Of course, the theological linkage of the Old and New Testament finds classical expression in the *munus triplex* of Jesus Christ as Priest, Prophet, and King.

In relation to this threefold office, we may describe *worship* as the center, where Christians are formed within the real, loving presence of God for participation in the mission of God, encountering again and again the inbreaking, prophetic Word of God in Jesus Christ through the power of the Holy Spirit. *Witness* is the outpouring of God's love for the world expressed in acts of love and care for neighbors, as Christians wrestle within the concrete personal, social, and political spheres of life with the wise, kingly Word of God in Jesus Christ, and as they are slowly and steadily turned from self-interest to self-giving through the power of the Holy Spirit. *Wonder* is the educational disposition of the church, as Christians explore Scripture and church teaching under the priestly mediation of the Word of God in Jesus Christ and in the power of the Holy Spirit.

The theological conviction and logic that underpinned catechesis in the early churches is clear: the Lord Jesus Christ himself, through the effectual operation of the Holy Spirit, continued to really be present in the church to teach, exhort, encourage, deliver from evil, convict of sin, forgive, and heal. In Israel, it was the prophet who had embodied and proclaimed the *pathos* of Yahweh for the wayward, forgetful covenant people. Now, the ministers of the church proclaimed the crucified, risen, and coming Christ to the community of the new covenant through the regular ministry of the Word and sacrament. The devotion of Christian faith was kindled, fanned into flame, and sustained over a lifetime through regular and active participation in the worship of the church, where Christ himself was really believed to be present.

Because of the fragmented subjectivist, activist, and objectivist emphases, American Protestants often reduce the *worship* of God to consumer-centered spiritual spectacle, ideological soapbox, or inflexible formalism; the *witness* to God's love of neighbor to offerings for "those who are less fortunate," political platforms, or handing out religious tracts; and the *wonder* accompanying the study, meditation, and interrogation of Scripture and church teaching to therapeutic remedies, political slogans, or absolute truth claims. In such a convoluted situation, it is little surprise that the positive public witness of the American Protestant churches today is less than overwhelming.

There is an interpretive tradition that sees Pentecost as the divine reversal of the Tower of Babel. Presumably, this would mean that at Pentecost the Holy Spirit gifted the church with a universal language. On the contrary, at the birth of the church described in Acts 2, the disheartened followers of Jesus are enabled by the Holy Spirit to speak about God's deeds of power, and listeners are able to understand what is being said *in their own native languages*. The multiplicity of languages, and by extension, the diversity of cultures, is blessed and overcome by the divine Spirit's gift! This story may help the church today move beyond the fragmenting tendencies of modern Protestantism. Why not imagine that each member of Christ's broken body, in his or her own imperfect way and limited cultural sphere, is, in the words of Karl Barth noted above in chapter 4, an "afflicted but well-equipped" witness to Jesus Christ under the agency of the Holy Spirit? Rather than pitting against each other the affective subjectivism of the more liberal churches, the volitional activism of the more progressive churches, or the cognitive objectivism of the more orthodox churches, why not boldly proclaim by faith that all of the churches, in their totality, together participate in and give witness to the divine/human praxis in Jesus Christ and the mission of God under the agency of the Holy Spirit?

In conclusion, I invite you to imagine the variant cultural perspectives and theologies of the World Christian movement as a massive flock of birds. Jan van IJken's beautiful film, which captures the fractal-like murmuration of huge flocks of starlings traversing space and time as a single body, is a fitting image of how such mind-boggling diversity may be preserved without any loss of unity. Notice that not a single bird falls or is pushed out of the airborne dance.[6] So, dear friends, as worshipers, witnesses, and wonderers moving from self-love to self-giving love of God and neighbor in the way of Jesus, let us learn again and again from the birds of the air and in the power of the Holy Spirit to murmurate and dance together as One, Holy, Catholic, and Apostolic Body of Christ!

6. See "Flight of the Starlings" on the National Geographic YouTube channel: https://www.youtube.com/watch?v=V4f_1_r80RY&ab_channel=National Geographic.

Postscript on Practical Theology and Catechesis

I BEGIN HERE WITH a personal story. Knowing that I had studied Christian education and practical theology, a very dedicated and busy American pastor friend once contacted me and asked me for a quick list of "the latest and the very best C.E. books for helping church school teachers." He went on, "I know that you have studied this area, and you must be knowledgeable of the current literature that can help our church school teachers teach kids more effectively. Just off the top of your head, give me a list. Oh yes, they've got to be practical, none of that theoretical gobbledygook, and easy to read!" I paused, giving this earnest pastor's question some thought. Yes, I knew of some good books that might be helpful, but I did not respond to his query immediately. Instead, I asked him some questions about the children who attended his church, their ages, prior experience in church school, family situations, economic level, whether they'd been baptized as infants or not, and so forth. Then I asked about the teachers, their ages, teaching experience, knowledge of children, the Bible, church doctrine, their church and faith experience, and so on. The pastor was clearly irritated by my questions. He responded, "What difference does all that matter? I thought you guys in Christian ed were supposed to be practical theologians!"

The point of this story is simple. From the beginning of the nineteenth century until quite recently, practical theology, the rubric under which Christian education (the classical term was catechesis) eventually fell within the modern seminary curriculum, was viewed as a kind of "applied theology" focusing on "how to" questions of application. Briefly, in the context of the emerging modern research-oriented university, theology, in keeping with the increasing specialization in other academic disciplines, was broken up into the four subdisciplines of biblical studies, church history, systematic theology (or dogmatics), and practical theology. As an organizational tool, this "encyclopedia" sought to relate each subdiscipline to the whole field.[1] Friedrich Schleiermacher, who pioneered this encyclopedia, in part as a way to safeguard a place for the study of theology within the modern university, originally offered a three-part division he called philosophical, historical, and practical theology. He believed that the task of philosophical and historical theology was "scientific," while the task of practical theology was oriented more toward technique (in an artistic sense). In both Schleiermacher's encyclopedia and today's more common fourfold division, practical theology was placed at the end of the course of study. This model is still common in seminary and divinity school curricula today.

Upon later reflection, it seems that this modern trend may have been a serious detour from the richer, classical understanding of practical reason that informed the catechesis of the early churches and the churches of the Reformation. According to Osmer, the classical view of practical reason combined both logic-centered and practical notions of reason and "was viewed as oriented toward the performance of a complex activity within a contingent field of experience . . . Reason was seen as moving analogically from paradigmatic to individual cases, providing help in how to perform such complex activities such as arguing a legal case, offering moral guidance, making a medical diagnosis or preaching a sermon."[2]

Of course, this notion of an acquired, "on-the-job" experiential wisdom (*sapientia*) is not an exclusively Greek notion.

1. Osmer, *Confirmation*, 220–28.

2. Osmer, *Confirmation*, 221.

Experiential wisdom is also highly regarded in places such as Japan, where apprenticeship traditions (*shokugyō kunren*) are very much alive and well, especially in traditional arts such as pottery, silk dying, painting, and the culinary arts.

Today, in professions such as medicine, law, and pastoral ministry that require academic and practical preparation, there is a growing interest in how to introduce the experiential dimension of practice into the curriculum at an earlier stage. Current medical education, for example, has recovered a more experiential-oriented approach by giving attention earlier on in the curriculum to direct patient care, albeit under the watchful eye of an experienced physician. Likewise, some seminaries and divinity schools are beginning to recognize a similar need to do more to help nurture this experiential wisdom in preparation for preaching and teaching ministries in the church.

In this book, I have tried to state the obvious again and again. Receiving and handing on the Gospel has never been, is not now, and will never be reducible to simple questions of method. In this complex process that incorporates theory and practice at every turn, we must face a wide range of issues concerning our particular views of Scripture, liturgy, ethics, missional calling and context, spirituality, and doctrine, as well as more obvious educational issues such as our educational philosophy, approach to teaching and learning, level of teacher commitment, and training. The view that biblical, historical, and systematic theologians set the parameters of the church's message (scientific theory) and practical theologians focus on how to preach or teach that message (technological practice) is a caricature of the much more complex process we actually discover when we consider how Christians in different times and places have received and passed on the Gospel.

In recent years, there has been much discussion about the nature of social practices, and catechesis may be examined as a particular social practice concerned with the transmission of Christian faith. Osmer points out that certain practices produce benefits "which cannot be gained in any other way than by participation in the practice. Certain knowledge and skills can only be acquired from the inside. Furthermore, only those who have acquired these things are competent to pass judgment when a practice is performed well."[3]

Osmer makes two other salient points about church practices: they are "narrative-dependent," and they have particular histories. "Narratives provide the cognitive framework in terms of which the goods engendered by practices are interpreted to and internalized by their participants." And to say that catechetical practices have particular histories is to say that they embody a long and broad "complex of meanings that are inherited from the past and socially shared in the present."[4] Naturally, the meaning of catechetical practices changes over time.

Early in the history of Christianity, "catechesis" became a technical term referring to prebaptismal instruction, and forms of the word are found in the New Testament, suggesting that some form of prebaptismal catechesis existed from a very early period (e.g., Gal 6:6; Acts 18:25). The word "catechesis" itself comes from the Greek *katēcheō*, which means "to resound," "sound through," "make hear," or "teach." T. F. Torrance says, "Through oral instruction the divine Word is made to sound in the ears of inquirers, enlightening their understanding and informing their life for Christian obedience."[5] John Westerhoff describes catechesis as "the process by which persons are initiated into the Christian community and its faith, revelation, and vocation; the process by which persons throughout their lifetimes are continually converted and nurtured, transformed and formed, by and in its living tradition."[6]

In this book, I have used "catechesis" broadly to refer to the many ways churches form, instruct, and nurture people "in Christ" for participation in God's mission in the world.[7] In my

3. Osmer, *Confirmation*, 29.

4. Osmer, *Confirmation*, 29–30.

5. Torrance, "Catechism," 85.

6. Westerhoff and Edwards, *Faithful Church*, 1.

7. As mentioned earlier, while "catechesis" is the classical term, and "Christian nurture" and "Christian education" were common in the nineteenth and twentieth centuries, "spiritual formation" and "discipleship" are used by various groups today to mean more or less the same thing.

view, the ultimate aim of catechesis is participation in the mission of God, expressed in the great commandments to love God and neighbor. Catechesis takes place in the *worship* of God, *witness* in all of the spheres of life, and *wonder*-filled study of Scripture, church teaching, theology, spiritual writings, and "parables of the kingdom" in the world.

As we saw in chapter 1, Torrance argues for a more scientific epistemology wherein the "self-disclosure" of the object under investigation always exercises a primary control over the inquirer.[8] In Christian faith, the self-revelation of the Subject of faith—the triune God, who comes to us in Jesus Christ and in the Holy Spirit—always exercises a primary, marginal control over the believer. This means there is an inescapable dimension of *pathos*, in the sense of an "undergoing," "suffering," or "bearing with," which cannot be avoided on the way to discovery, insight, and transformation. In terms of James Loder's logic of transformation, *pathos* is brought to a new depth and intensity in the second movement, the *interlude for scanning,* where new insight is waiting to break in upon the knower, but where also the downward psychic drive toward social or ideological conformity is often overpowering.[9]

In terms of the participation in God's mission "in Christ," which is the ultimate goal of catechesis, *pathic self-giving* may be understood using an analogy to the silent and painful "in-between time" after Good Friday and before Easter Sunday. From the sealed tomb and the "descent into hell," all seemed lost, and the triumph of nonbeing, unequivocal. Like Jesus, those who are being formed and transformed "in Christ" learn that there is no escaping "Holy Saturday" on the way to Easter light. For Christians, the divine mediation that negates negation, delivering "death to death," is forever cruciform. There is no empty tomb without the cross. The cross *and* the resurrection, not one without the other, provide the ground of the *participatio Christi. Pathic self-giving* is the hope-filled attitude of all who, in baptism,

8. See discussion of brain cells in chapter 1.

9. Loder, *Transforming Moment.*

have put on the crucified and risen Lord, who is revealed in self-giving love for God and neighbor.

While the recent scholarly and ecclesial interest in catechesis reflects a positive acknowledgment of the need for a more holistic approach to Christian formation, this interest is not an unambiguous development in our North American context. This ambivalence is captured well by theologian George Lindbeck in the final chapter of his book, *The Nature of Doctrine*. On the one hand, Lindbeck says that his "postliberal, cultural-linguistic" approach to doctrine "resembles ancient catechesis more than modern translation. Instead of redescribing the faith in new concepts, it seeks to teach the language and practices of the religion to potential adherents." On the other hand, Lindbeck was pessimistic about any practical application of his proposal in the current sociocultural situation of North America.

> Western culture is now at an intermediate stage, however, where socialization is ineffective, catechesis impossible, and translation a tempting alternative. . . . The intertextual intelligibility that postliberalism emphasizes may not fit the needs of religions such as Christianity when they are in the awkward intermediate stage of having once been culturally established but are not yet clearly disestablished.

Lindbeck leaves the reader with the paradoxical (Lutheran?) conclusion that, while postliberalism may bear a family resemblance to the catechesis of the early church, a renewal of catechesis is ruled out, because the churches today are so completely enculturated. "In the present situation, unlike periods of missionary expansion, the churches primarily accommodate to the prevailing culture rather than shape it."[10]

While conceding his point about the Western churches, since Lindbeck was the son of Lutheran missionaries and grew up in China and Korea, I only wish he had mentioned that, as a matter of fact, there are many places in the world today that are experiencing "missionary expansion." Indeed, the present book comes out of my

10. Lindbeck, *Nature of Doctrine*, 132–33.

years of teaching in Japan, and I will not be surprised if my work finds more resonance in such places than in North America.[11]

11. This postscript is written with sincere gratitude to James E. Loder and Richard R. Osmer, my doctoral advisers in practical theology at Princeton Theological Seminary.

APPENDIX

Additional Thoughts on Worship, Witness, and Wonder across the Ages

Worship

Ancient Catholic Churches: Liturgical Initiation

In the ancient catholic churches, the sense of being beloved of God and loving God was awakened, sustained, and renewed through participation in the liturgical practices of the community of faith. For early church catechumens, this included initiation into a wide range of ritual practices, including the reading, hearing, and explication of Scripture in corporate worship, public and private prayer, private meditation on the Creed, the Lord's Prayer, exorcisms, fasting, vigils, and so forth.

Medieval Churches: The Mass as Sacrament

In the churches of medieval Europe, the sense of being beloved of God and loving God was awakened, sustained, and renewed through weekly or (during festival times) daily participation in the Mass and a range of associated devotional practices (novenas, fasting, shrine pilgrimage, rosary, etc.).

Reformation Churches: Word and Sacrament

In the Reformation churches, the sense of being beloved of God and loving God was awakened, sustained, and renewed through attendance at public services of worship focused on the reading and explication of Scripture, daily prayer patterned on the Lord's Prayer, and participating in the sacraments of baptism and the Lord's Supper.

Modern Protestant Churches: Church Membership and Personal Conversion

In the modern Protestant churches, the sense of being beloved of God and loving God is awakened, sustained, and renewed through regular attendance at public services of worship where Scripture is read and explicated, with an emphasis on an experience of personal conversion (usually as a public, affective expression of faith) and devotional practice (private prayer and Bible reading/study).

In all four paradigms, the *pathos* of God that infuses communal and personal faith was regularly renewed, primarily within the various public contexts of worship and, secondarily, in a range of private devotional practices. Note the close conjunction of affective perception and cognitive reflection here. Potentially transformational moments in the divine presence and within the gathered community of faith complement the more obviously "educational" or formational work of teaching and learning the *ethos* of the Gospel. Just as the Law and Prophets are indispensable partners in Israel's faith, so the Gospel is inextricably bound to the public and private worship of God in the formation and transformation of Christian communities.

I need to sound a note of caution here, because there has probably been more confusion and conflict concerning the worship of God than any other facet of the Christian religious life. We know, for example, that the Christian communities in front of the New Testament texts engaged in a variety of worship practices that drew mostly on Jewish but also on Greco-Roman ideas and traditions.

This was increasingly the case as the churches developed within Greco-Roman religious environments. There was likely a wide variety of local worship styles. Several texts in the New Testament point to serious tensions within the earliest Christian communities concerning the proper worship of God. For example, from First Corinthians 12–14, we learn that there was considerable confusion in the Corinthian community about the proper balance between public order and personal devotion in worship.

In this book, I claim that the worship of God is an integral aspect of and not a simple adjunct to the church's educational vocation of receiving and handing on the Gospel of the self-giving love of God in Jesus Christ, but I do not mean primarily in the instrumental, pragmatic sense that mechanically links certain religious practices (e.g., the oral recitation of a confession of sin) to some religious "good" or "outcome" (e.g., a renewed consciousness of forgiveness of sins). By speaking of the worship of God as the Christian analogue to prophecy in Israel, I hope to draw our attention beyond the arguments concerning form, order, disposition, and pragmatic instrumentality to a prior and more significant reality. Just as prophetic utterance in Israel is typically uncredentialed, free, and unsettling, Christian worship is also centered more on the present, inbreaking disruption of Word and sacrament than on questions of form, order, disposition, or "goods-producing," theory-laden practices. The core perception that the community of faith gathers in the real presence of Jesus Christ, who, through the power of the Holy Spirit, continues to speak through Word and sacrament, renewing the community's being and identity in God, moving a community from self-love to self-giving love of God and neighbor. This core theological convictional about worship relativizes all psychological, sociological, or anthropological considerations about what "happens" in worship.

As far as I can discern, Paul's pastoral, evangelical concern in First Corinthians 12–14 seems to be that no particular custom of the community be allowed to obstruct the convictional, transformational, and converting agency of God in the worship event. His argument against speaking in tongues in the gathered assembly, for example, is an evangelical concern for "outsiders or unbelievers" (1 Cor 14:23) more than either a prohibition or endorsement of displays of religious ecstasy. His desire is that these visitors will recognize that "God is really among you" (1 Cor 14:25b). Just as prophecy inspires the renewal of a dynamic, subversive, and alternative identity to the "royal consciousness" in Israel, so Christian worship centers on the Gospel proclamation of repentance, forgiveness of sin, and reception of the gift of the Holy Spirit, who renews a people again and again. Just as Israel needed the prompting of prophets to call them home to their core identity, so the church needs faithful and subversive preachers of the Word to unsettle and resettle the community's sense of being and belonging in the presence of divine love.

Witness

Ancient Catholic Churches: Moral Examination and Exhortation

In the ancient catholic churches, the Christian way of life was regularly communicated through moral examination and exhortation. For catechumens, this included interrogations of personal motives, lifestyle, and vocation, with appeals to see one's life and vocation to love one's neighbor anew through the baptismal pattern of "dying and rising" in and with Christ.

Medieval Churches: Confession, Penance, and Absolution

In the medieval churches of Europe, the Christian way of life was regularly communicated in the presence and authority of a priest through a process of self-examination, penance, and the granting of absolution.

Reformation Churches: Ten Commandments

In the Reformation churches, the Christian way of life was communicated through public confession of sin and assurance of forgiveness and didactic interpretations of the Ten Commandments as a practical guide for life *coram Deo* ("before/in the face of/in the presence of God").

Modern Protestant Churches: Social Reconstruction

In the modern Protestant churches, the Christian way of life is communicated through teaching that encourages participation in movements seeking a society that more faithfully reflects the values of the kingdom of God.

With varying emphases, in all four eras the churches tried to make explicit the ethical imperatives of the Gospel and, as witnesses to what God has done in Jesus Christ, to teach how to apply the ethical imperatives of the Gospel to private and public life. The movement from *worship* to *witness* is always a risky business, and as history plainly shows, churches have sinned whenever the Gospel has been used to impose "objective" ethical standards, justify sectarian claims of holiness, and endorse other kinds of psychological, social, or political oppression. In spite of the risk of abusing the ethical imperatives of the Gospel, Christians have always felt called to engage contemporary ethical and moral issues, as well as to take seriously the call to personally respond to the Gospel. As with the Old Testament Writings, which articulate Israel's best hunches about how to live in the light of the Torah, there is always a tentativeness to the ethical discernments of the churches as they seek to give witness to the Gospel of Jesus Christ.

Wonder

Ancient Catholic Churches: Baptismal Catechesis

In the ancient catholic churches, the Gospel of Jesus Christ was transmitted and received through the time-intensive process of baptismal catechesis. Baptismal catechesis here refers to the pedagogical process of orally handing on Scripture and church teaching to adult converts. The catechesis was commonly delivered by bishops, priests, or deacons to adult candidates for baptism and organized around a sustained rhetorical presentation of the articles of a particular creed as the symbol of faith grounded in and supported by Scripture.

Medieval Churches: Evocative Use of Christian Symbols

In the medieval churches of Europe, the Gospel of Jesus Christ was transmitted and received through the regular, embodied apprehension (visual, auditory, tactile, and olfactory) of a rich range of Christian objects and symbols used in church architecture, sculpture, paintings, liturgies, hymnody, hagiography, cyclical festivals, passion plays, and similar events.

Reformation Churches: Study of the Apostles' Creed

In the Reformation churches, the Gospel of Jesus Christ was transmitted and received through the systematic study of some interpretation of the Apostles' Creed, which was the focus of the catechisms used primarily in families, but also in churches and schools.

Modern Protestant Churches: Socialization/Enculturation

In the modern Protestant churches, the Gospel of Jesus Christ is transmitted and received through socialization into the faith of a community and into a community of faith. This involves study of age-appropriate and relevant portions of Scripture and/or church doctrine as outlined in catechisms.

With varying emphases, in all four eras there is a common emphasis on teaching (1) the biblical stories of Israel and Jesus Christ and (2) church doctrine. Note the close conjunction of Scripture and confession of faith. If Torah provides the basis for knowledge of God, confession of faith, and religious identity in Israel, the story of Israel and the church's interpretation of Jesus Christ provide the basis for the knowledge of God, confession of faith, and religious identity in the Christian community. Just as the Torah encompasses the inexhaustibly rich strands of the biblical narrative and intracanonical traditions of theological interpretation in Israel, the Gospel similarly encompasses the stories of Jesus and the core confession of Jesus as the Christ within the communities of faith in front of the diverse writings of the New Testament.

Bibliography

Allen, Joseph L. *Love and Conflict: A Covenantal Model of Christian Ethics.* Lanham: University Press of America, 1995.

Astley, Jeff. "The Role of Worship in Christian Learning." In *Theological Perspectives on Christian Formation,* edited by Jeff Astley, Leslie J. Francis, and Colin Crowder, 244–51. Grand Rapids: Eerdmans, 1996.

Barth, Karl. *Church Dogmatics.* Vol. 4. Edited by Geoffrey W. Bromiley and Thomas F. Torrance. Edinburgh: T&T Clark, 1956.

Bauer, Walter. *A Greek-English Lexicon of the New Testament and Other Early Christian Literature.* Edited by W. F. Arndt and F. W. Gingrich. Chicago: University of Chicago Press, 1979.

Berntsen, John. "Christian Affections and the Catechumenate." In *Theological Perspectives on Christian Formation,* edited by Jeff Astley, Leslie J. Francis, and Colin Crowder, 229–43. Grand Rapids: Eerdmans, 1996.

Berger, Peter L., and Thomas Luckmann. *The Social Construction of Reality: A Treatise in the Sociology of Knowledge.* New York: Anchor, 1966.

Bettensen, Henry, ed. *The Early Christian Fathers.* Oxford: Oxford University Press, 1956.

Bornkamm, Gunther. *Paul.* Translated by D. M. G. Stalker. New York: Harper & Row, 1969.

Brueggemann, Walter. *The Creative Word: Canon as a Model for Biblical Education.* Philadelphia: Fortress, 1982.

Calvin, John. *Institutes of the Christian Religion.* Edited by John T. McNeill. Louisville: Westminster John Knox, 1960.

Center for Liturgical Research. *Made, Not Born: New Perspectives on Christian Initiation and the Catechumenate.* Notre Dame: University of Notre Dame Press, 1976.

Chadwick, Henry. *The Early Church.* London: Penguin, 1967.

Cyril of Alexandria. *Catechetical Lecture.* In *Nicene and Post-Nicene Fathers,* edited by Philip Schaff and Henry Wace, 1–157. Buffalo: Christian Literature, 1894.

Dean, Kenda, et al. *Consensus and Conflict: Practical Theology for Congregations in the Work of Richard R. Osmer*. Eugene, OR: Cascade, 2019.

Dudley, Carl S., and Earle Hilgert. *New Testament Tensions and the Contemporary Church*. Philadelphia: Fortress, 1987.

Dykstra, Craig R., and Sharon Parks, eds. *Faith Development and Fowler*. Birmingham: Religious Education, 1986.

Edwards, O. C. "The New Testament Church: From Jesus to the Apologists." In *A Faithful Church: Issues in the History of Catechesis*, edited by John Westerhoff III and O. C. Edwards, 10–48. Wilton: Morehouse-Barlow, 1981.

Egeria. *Travels*. Translated by John Wilkinson. London: SPCK, 1971.

Eisner, Elliot. *The Educational Imagination: On the Design and Evaluation of School Programs*. New York: Macmillan, 1979.

Ferguson, Everett, ed. *Conversion, Catechumenate, and Baptism in the Early Church*. New York: Garland, 1993.

Folkemer, Lawrence D. "A Study of the Catechumenate." In *Conversion, Cathechumenate, and Baptism in the Early Church*, edited by Everett Ferguson, 244–65. New York: Garland, 1993.

Fowler, James W. *Stages of Faith: The Psychology of Human Development and the Quest for Meaning*. San Francisco: Harper & Row, 1981.

Fowler, James W., et al. *Life Maps: Conversations on the Journey of Faith*. Waco: Word, 1978.

Fox, Robin Lane. *Pagans and Christians*. New York: Knopf, 1987.

Geertz, Clifford. *The Interpretation of Cultures*. New York: Basic, 1973.

Groome, Thomas. *Christian Religious Education: Sharing Our Story and Vision*. San Francisco: Harper & Row, 1980.

Hastings, Thomas John. *Practical Theology and the One Body of Christ: Toward a Missional-Ecumenical Model*. Grand Rapids: Eerdmans, 2007.

Hippolytus of Rome. *The Apostolic Tradition*. Edited by Gregory Dix and Henry Chadwick. London: SPCK, 1968.

Hunsinger, George. *Disruptive Grace: Studies in the Theology of Karl Barth*. Grand Rapids: Eerdmans, 2000.

Irenaeus of Lyons. *Against Heresies*. In vol. 3, *Ante-Nicene Fathers*, edited by Alexander Roberts and James Donaldson, 309–567. Peabody: Hendrickson, 1995.

Isaacson, Walter, ed. *A Ben Franklin Reader*. New York: Simon & Schuster, 2003.

Kelly, J. N. D. *Early Christian Creeds*. London: Longman, 1972.

Kierkegaard, Søren. *The Journals of Kierkegaard: A Selection*. Edited and translated by Alexander Dru. London: Oxford University Press, 1938.

———. *Works of Love*. New York: Harper Torchbooks, 1962.

Lehmann, Paul. *Ethics in a Christian Context*. New York: Harper & Row, 1963.

Lifton, Robert Jay. *The Protean Self: Human Resilience in an Age of Fragmentation*. Chicago: University of Chicago Press, 1993.

Lindbeck, George. *The Nature of Doctrine: Religion and Theology in a Postliberal Age*. Philadelphia: Westminster, 1984.

Loder, James E. *The Transforming Moment*. Colorado Springs: Helmers & Howard, 1989.

Marrou, H. I. *A History of Education in Antiquity*. Madison: University of Wisconsin Press, 1956.

Niebuhr, H. Richard. *Responsible Self*. New York: Harper & Row, 1963.

———. *The Purpose of the Church and Its Ministry*. New York: Harper & Row, 1956.

Newbigin, Lesslie. *Proper Confidence: Faith, Doubt, and Certainty in Christian Discipleship*. Grand Rapids: Eerdmans, 1995.

Office of the General Assembly. *The Constitution of the Presbyterian Church (USA)*. Pt. 2, *The Book of Order*. Louisville: Office of the General Assembly, 2004.

———. "The Scots Confession." In *The Constitution of the Presbyterian Church (USA)*, pt. 1: *The Book of Confessions*, 9–26. Louisville: Office of the General Assembly, 2014.

Osmer, Richard Robert. *Confirmation: Presbyterian Practice in Ecumenical Perspective*. Louisville: Geneva, 1996.

———. *The Teaching Ministry of Congregations*. Louisville: Westminster John Knox, 2005.

Paxton, Robert O. *The Anatomy of Fascism*. New York: Knopf, 2004.

Polanyi, Michael. *Personal Knowing: Towards a Post-critical Philosophy*. Chicago: University of Chicago Press, 1958.

Ricoeur, Paul. *Interpretation Theory: Discourse and the Surplus of Meaning*. Fort Worth: Texas Christian University Press, 1979.

Roberts, Alexander, and James Donaldson, eds. *Ante-Nicene Fathers*. 10 vols. Peabody: Hendrickson, 1995.

Schaff, Philip, and Henry Wace, eds. *Nicene and Post-Nicene Fathers, Second Series*. Buffalo: Christian Literature, 1894.

Seymour, Jack L. *Contemporary Approaches to Christian Education*. Nashville: Abingdon, 1982.

Small, Joseph D. "Changing Times." *Hungry Hearts* 15.3 (2006) 3.

Smart, James D. *The Teaching Ministry of the Church*. Philadelphia: Westminster, 1954.

Stark, Rodney. *The Rise of Christianity: How the Obscure, Marginal Jesus Movement Became the Dominant Religious Force in the Western World in a Few Centuries*. Princeton: Princeton University Press, 1996.

Teaching of the Twelve Apostles. In vol. 7, *Ante-Nicene Fathers*, edited by Alexander Roberts and James Donaldson, 377–82. Peabody: Hendrickson, 1995.

Tillich, Paul. *Systematic Theology*. Vol. 3, *Life and the Spirit: History and the Kingdom of God*. Chicago: University of Chicago Press, 1963.

Torrance, Thomas F. "Catechism." In *Westminster Dictionary of Christian Education*, edited by Kendig Brubaker Cully, 85–88. Philadelphia: Westminster, 1963.

———. *The Doctrine of Grace in the Apostolic Fathers*. Edinburgh: Oliver & Boyd, 1948.

———. *The Mediation of Christ*. Colorado Springs: Helmers & Howard, 1992.

———. *The School of Faith*. New York: Harper & Brothers, 1959.

———. *Theological Science*. Edinburgh: T&T Clark, 1969.

Turner, Cuthbert Hamilton. *The History and Use of Creeds and Anathemas in the Early Centuries of the Church*. London: SPCK, 1906.

Walls, Andrew. "The Expansion of Christianity: An Interview with Andrew Walls." *Christian Century* 117.22 (August 2–9, 2000) 792–95.

Westerhoff, John H., III. *Will Our Children Have Faith?* New York: Seabury, 1976.

Westerhoff, John H., III, and O. C. Edwards, eds. *A Faithful Church: Issues in the History of Catechesis*. Wilton: Morehouse-Barlow, 1981.

Yeats, W. B. *The Collected Poems*. New York: Macmillan, 1972.